# 11+ Verbal Reasoning
# Vocabulary

## For the **CEM** test

For success in the CEM 11+, you're going to need great vocabulary skills, so we've made this superb book of 10-Minute Tests for pupils aged 9-10.

It's jam-packed with realistic practice to improve word power, plus answers and a handy progress chart at the back of the book!

# 10-Minute Tests

### Ages
## 9-10

---

### How to access your free **Online Edition**

This book includes a free Online Edition to read on your PC, Mac or tablet.
You'll just need to go to **cgpbooks.co.uk/extras** and enter this code:

## 2260 0493 8591 2786

By the way, this code only works for one person. If somebody else has used this book before you, they might have already claimed the Online Edition.

# How to use this book

This book is made up of 10-minute tests and puzzle pages.
There are answers at the back of the book.

## 10-Minute Tests

- There are 31 tests in this book, each containing 25 questions.

- Each test is designed to target the type of vocabulary questions that your child
  could come across in the verbal reasoning section of their 11+ test.

- Your child should aim to score at least 21 out of 25 in each of the 10-minute tests.
  If they score less than this, use their results to work out the areas they need more practice on.

- If your child hasn't managed to finish the test in time, they need to work on increasing their
  speed, whereas if they have made a lot of mistakes, they need to work more carefully.

- Keep track of your child's scores using the progress chart on the last page of the book.

## Puzzle Pages

- There are 12 puzzle pages in this book, which are a great break from test-style questions.
  They encourage children to practise the skills that they will need in the test, but in a fun way.

Published by CGP

Editors:
Andy Cashmore, Eleanor Claringbold, Emma Cleasby, Robbie Driscoll, Emily Forsberg, Melissa Gardner,
Kelsey Hammond, Becca Lakin, James Summersgill

With thanks to Holly Robinson for the proofreading.

Please note that CGP is not associated with CEM in any way.
This book does not include any official questions and it is not endorsed by CEM.

ISBN: 978 1 78908 439 9
Printed by Elanders Ltd, Newcastle upon Tyne
Clipart from Corel®

Based on the classic CGP style created by Richard Parsons.

Text, design, layout and original illustrations © Coordination Group Publications Ltd. (CGP) 2019
All rights reserved.

Photocopying this book is not permitted, even if you have a CLA licence.
Extra copies are available from CGP with next day delivery. • 0800 1712 712 • www.cgpbooks.co.uk

# Contents

You have **10 minutes** to do this test.  Work as quickly and as accurately as you can.

> Underline the correct homophone to complete the sentence.
>
> **Example**: Archie tied a _____ in the ship's rigging.    not  <u>knot</u>

1.  Lindsay said we _____ some milk.                    knead   need

2.  Preena was enjoying the school _____.               fate   fête

3.  Tim's _____ didn't taste very nice.                 steak   stake

4.  Rahul found a _____ in his bathroom pipes.          leak   leek

5.  Max baked the _____ to turn it into bread.          doe   dough

6.  Emily _____ at the sad movie.                       bawled   bald

> Find the word that is a synonym, or nearly a synonym, of the word on the left.
>
> **Example**: **wide**    flat   straight   <u>broad</u>   long

7.  **past**        sinking   bygone   uncharted   forlorn

8.  **harbour**     yacht   sandcastle   anvil   anchorage

9.  **employee**    student   recruiter   founder   worker

10. **ooze**        stink   sag   seep   reveal

11. **likeness**    view   resemblance   delegate   mirror

12. **expansion**   greatness   obsession   flight   extension

Choose the correct three-letter word to complete the word in capital letters, so that it finishes the sentence in a sensible way.

**Example**: It can be **CHY** outside when it snows.

| APP | ILL | EEK | ERR |
|:---:|:---:|:---:|:---:|
| ☐ | ▬ | ☐ | ☐ |

13. We tried to keep the new puppy off the white **CARS**.

| USE | ROT | PET | TON |
|:---:|:---:|:---:|:---:|
| ☐ | ☐ | ☐ | ☐ |

14. Isla clung on as her horse broke into a **CER**.

| HAS | ALL | ANT | RAT |
|:---:|:---:|:---:|:---:|
| ☐ | ☐ | ☐ | ☐ |

15. Samira **MED** up some banana and fed it to her little sister.

| ASH | ARK | AIM | ILK |
|:---:|:---:|:---:|:---:|
| ☐ | ☐ | ☐ | ☐ |

16. Ben couldn't find the potato **PER** anywhere.

| AND | OUR | EEL | LAY |
|:---:|:---:|:---:|:---:|
| ☐ | ☐ | ☐ | ☐ |

17. Her class said she would be **SLY** missed.

| ORE | OUR | LOW | MUG |
|:---:|:---:|:---:|:---:|
| ☐ | ☐ | ☐ | ☐ |

18. Lola tried to avoid **CRING** into her friends while running around.

| AMP | ASH | APE | OAK |
|:---:|:---:|:---:|:---:|
| ☐ | ☐ | ☐ | ☐ |

19. The police officer was **SPING** the traffic.

| END | ARK | ILL | TOP |
|:---:|:---:|:---:|:---:|
| ☐ | ☐ | ☐ | ☐ |

Complete the word on the right so that it is an antonym,
or nearly an antonym, of the word on the left.

**Example**: smooth [r][o][u][g][h]

20. visible [ ][i][d][ ][ ][n]

21. notice [o][v][ ][r][l][ ][o][ ]

22. free [i][ ][p][r][ ][s][ ][n][ ][d]

23. unforeseen [ ][x][ ][e][c][ ][e][d]

24. untested [p][ ][ ][v][ ][n]

25. clamp [ ][n][f][ ][ ][t][ ][n]

**END OF TEST**

/ 25

4

© CGP — not to be photocopied

You have **10 minutes** to do this test.  Work as quickly and as accurately as you can.

Three of the words in each list are linked.  Mark the word that is not related to these three.

**Example**: teacher   doctor   <u>hospital</u>   firefighter

1.  whisker   talon   hoof   claw

2.  brooch   necklace   accessory   ring

3.  carrot   orange   apricot   beetroot

4.  pelican   warthog   hyena   meerkat

5.  airship   helipad   rocket   aeroplane

Find the word that is an antonym, or nearly an antonym, of the word on the left.

**Example**: **first**   later   <u>last</u>   next   beginning

6.  **lessened**   turned   amplified   mimed   deafened

7.  **release**   hunt   ease   deliver   ensnare

8.  **descent**   origin   ascension   clamber   failure

9.  **small**   moderate   extensive   shrinking   singular

10. **voluntary**   advisory   defenceless   compulsory   vital

Select the most appropriate word from the table to complete each pair of synonyms below.  Write the word on the corresponding line.

| enduring | veiled | alleviate | bitter | appreciate |
| obstruction | surpassed | tuneful | indignantly | refusal |

11. outdid        _____

12. resentful      _____

13. long-lasting  _____

14. denial         _____

15. melodic        _____

16. concealed    _____

17. angrily        _____

18. soothe         _____

19. understand   _____

20. blockage      _____

Mark the word outside the brackets that has a similar meaning to the words in both sets of brackets.

**Example**: (find  discover)  (stain  blemish)     freckle   smudge   <u>spot</u>   see

21. (obvious  evident)    (staring  scowling)    glaring  looking  lucid  watering

22. (exact  right)        (fix  rectify)         impose  request  correct  precise

23. (torso  body)         (chest  case)          crate  trunk  frame  casket

24. (shelter  protect)    (sleeve  wrapper)      cover  cushion  haven  film

25. (stair  tread)        (phase  stage)         section  step  pace  tier

**END OF TEST**

/ 25

                        © CGP — not to be photocopied

# Puzzles 1

Time for a break!  This puzzle is a great way to practise your **word-making** skills.

# Fishing for Words

The letters in the water below can be used to make lots of different words.  Rearrange the letters to make words, and write them down under each heading below. Keep going until you've filled in all of the lines. Each letter can only be used once per word.

There is also one nine-letter word to find.

3-letter words:

_____
_____
_____
_____
_____
_____

4-letter words:

_____
_____
_____
_____
_____
_____

I L H O P O R L P W

5-letter words:

_____
_____

6-letter words:

_____
_____

Can you find the nine-letter word? _____
(Hint: it means a swirling pool of water.)

© CGP — not to be photocopied

7

Puzzles 1

You have **10 minutes** to do this test. Work as quickly and as accurately as you can.

Underline a word from the first set, followed by a word from the second set, that go together to form a new word.

**Example**: (<u>water</u> suggest disc) (<u>fall</u> hard ton)   (The word is **waterfall**.)

1.  (crush  hoarse  in)          (shed  stall  pound)

2.  (care  sun  tall)            (city  country  light)

3.  (head  face  nose)          (straight  line  curve)

4.  (down  lard  butter)        (end  pot  cup)

5.  (at  across  side)           (date  ways  year)

6.  (pause  break  snap)        (crouch  down  duck)

7.  (crash  drum  beat)         (mark  branch  stick)

Underline the word that is the best antonym for the word in bold and makes sense in the sentence.

**Example**: Peter found the visit **dull**.        <u>exciting</u>  dreary  upsetting  boring

8.  Vidar thought the waiter was very **uncooperative**.

    dim  impolite  generous  helpful

9.  Emma couldn't **fasten** her shoes.

    shut  unbuckle  slow  disentangle

8                    © CGP — not to be photocopied

10. Billy watched the **incoming** plane circle the airport.

    outrunning    outgoing    overtaking    quitting

11. The girl had some very **extraordinary** stamps in her collection.

    unremarkable    traditional    impressive    uncanny

12. I decided to **relinquish** my new football on one condition.

    abandon    keep    purchase    forego

13. My sister explained in great detail the **merits** of owning a cat.

    obstacles    disadvantages    distractions    bonuses

Complete the word on the right so that it is a synonym,
or nearly a synonym, of the word on the left.

**Example**: rug    c a r p e t

14. prosper    ☐ h r ☐ v e

15. chaos    d ☐ ☐ o ☐ d ☐ r

16. covertly    s ☐ c ☐ e ☐ l y

17. related    ☐ o n ☐ ☐ c ☐ e d

18. discourage    d ☐ s h ☐ ☐ r t ☐ n

19. hate    d ☐ s p ☐ s ☐

9

Look at the word on the left.  Underline the category that it belongs to.

**Example**:  **scarlet**    <u>red</u>   yellow   blue   green

20.  mansion          house       bungalow       skyscraper       office

21.  copper           plastic      wood        surface       metal

22.  fury             instinct      irritation       tantrum       emotion

23.  butter           cheese       knife       spread       nutrition

24.  magician         illusion       wand       performer       ploy

25.  marble           building       stone       glass       wall

**END OF TEST**

/ 25

                                    © CGP — not to be photocopied

You have **10 minutes** to do this test.  Work as quickly and as accurately as you can.

> Three of the words in each list are linked.  Mark the word that is not related to these three.
>
> **Example**: teacher   doctor   <u>hospital</u>   firefighter

1.  yoghurt   milk   cream   juice

2.  steadfast   dependable   disloyal   trustworthy

3.  blanket   duvet   carpet   quilt

4.  glue   bind   ruler   stick

5.  medal   conquest   trophy   prize

6.  fort   prison   gaol   jail

> Underline the correct homophone to complete the sentence.
>
> **Example**: Archie tied a _____ in the ship's rigging.    not   <u>knot</u>

7.  Last year, we _____ to Australia.         flew   flu

8.  I turn off my laptop so I don't _____ electricity.    waist   waste

9.  The lion has the loudest _____ in the zoo.    raw   roar

10. I eat food slowly so I can _____ it.    savour   saver

11. Niamh's brother thinks she is lazy and _____.    idol   idle

12. The bank gave Josef a _____ for his business.     lone   loan

13. Kay tried to _____ the dog away.     shoo   shoe

---

Underline the word that is the best synonym for the word in bold and makes sense in the sentence.

**Example**: The river was **broad**.     flowing   muddy   <u>wide</u>   fast

---

14. Anita's teacher was very **self-assured** in the classroom.
    assertive   condescending   professional   reassuring

15. The king **exploits** his power and treats his citizens badly.
    mocks   misunderstands   abuses   ignores

16. The visitor was wearing an unusual set of **clothes**.
    outfitters   wardrobes   kits   garments

17. Lesley's history book is completely **captivating**.
    uninformative   numbing   releasing   enthralling

18. My grandma gave me a **sizeable** amount of money.
    unforgettable   considerable   agreeable   knowable

19. The boy put a **bundle** of papers onto the fire.
    box   bunch   lump   receptacle

Look at the definition on the left.  Underline the word on the right that best matches the definition.

**Example**:  to jog slowly          scurry    lunge    sprint    <u>trot</u>

20.  to hug closely          jostle    welcome    clench    <u>embrace</u>

21.  to harvest a crop       plant    sow    <u>reap</u>    water

22.  help or assistance      supervision    <u>aid</u>    management    caution

23.  to put a stop to        diminish    dismiss    <u>terminate</u>    commit

24.  to fall quickly         soar    <u>plummet</u>    swim    levitate

25.  to lengthen             <u>elongate</u>    modify    transform    bend

## END OF TEST

/ 25

It's break time!  Have a go at this puzzle to practise your **vocabulary** skills.

# Treasure Trail Teaser

Isabel is on a treasure hunt, but she needs your help to find the treasure.  Solve the clues and fill in the crossword below.  Then, unscramble the letters in the blue boxes to find the location of the treasure.

**Across clues**

1. where you sleep

6. unsettled

7. the place where a pig lives

9. smallest

10. paying attention

11. teach one student

12. clothes worn to school

13. an animal kept at home

15. a word that means 'certain'

16. a space in something

**Down clues**

1. a way of getting around

2. it has twenty-four hours

3. go to see someone

4. the highest amount possible

5. where the land meets the ocean

8. very skilful

9. the vehicles moving along a road

11. a vehicle that follows tracks

13. a clip used to hang clothes

14. the pointy end of a pen

Location of the treasure: _ _ _ _ _ / _ _ _ / _ _ _ _ _ _ _

Hint: the first word means the opposite of 'over'.

 © CGP — not to be photocopied

10

You have **10 minutes** to do this test.  Work as quickly and as accurately as you can.

> Underline a word from the first set, followed by a word from the second set, that go together to form a new word.
>
> **Example**: (<u>water</u> suggest disc) (<u>fall</u> hard ton)   (The word is **waterfall**.)

1.  (pull  for  sit)        (stay  get  die)

2.  (stand  fall  bar)      (din  low  by)

3.  (arm  car  do)          (rage  grow  pet)

4.  (con  man  cat)         (age  line  track)

5.  (short  shape  show)    (on  case  top)

6.  (taste  hard  pan)      (tree  less  full)

> Look at the word on the left.  Underline the category that it belongs to.
>
> **Example**:  scarlet          <u>red</u>    yellow    blue    green

7.  kayak          paddle    boat    sport    steamer

8.  Welsh          country    territory    person    language

9.  tutor          teacher    student    learning    lesson

10. basement       aisle    level    attic    dungeon

11. hotel          home    accommodation    lodge    holiday

12. pork           pig    sausage    taste    meat

> Complete the word on the right so that it is an antonym,
> or nearly an antonym, of the word on the left.
>
> **Example**: smooth     r <u>oug</u> h

13. violent       pea_____l

14. commence       _____ish

15. bury       un_____th

16. fascinating       du_____

17. unsuccessful       eff_____ive

18. unfriendly       appr_____hable

19. shrink       en_____ge

> Underline the word that is the best synonym for the word in bold and makes
> sense in the sentence.
>
> **Example**: The river was **broad**.     flowing   muddy   <u>wide</u>   fast

20. To most people, Tabitha seemed like an **ordinary** little girl.
    unrecognised   dominant   unexceptional   excitable

21. The mayor provided a **substantial** amount of money for the project.
    startling   standard   paltry   significant

22. The injury was painful, but there wasn't any **permanent** damage.
    lasting   serious   actual   excruciating

23. The gallery was full of artists **exhibiting** their work.

    selling    displaying    destroying    describing

24. The crime was witnessed by a group of **bystanders**.

    guards    accomplices    policemen    onlookers

25. Anirudh had to use all his brainpower to **decipher** the puzzle.

    contemplate    unlace    encrypt    solve

**END OF TEST**

/ 25

You have **10 minutes** to do this test.  Work as quickly and as accurately as you can.

> Underline a word from the first set, followed by a word from the second set, that go together to form a new word.
>
>   **Example**: (<u>water</u> suggest disc) (<u>fall</u> hard ton)   (The word is **waterfall**.)

1.   (hat  pie  time)          (rest  table  rate)

2.   (break  high  bee)        (cage  way  live)

3.   (far  enter  war)         (ten  fair  lock)

4.   (go  trip  vile)          (odd  let  sing)

5.   (bar  end  hum)           (rum  our  ill)

> Look at the definition on the left.  Underline the word on the right that best matches the definition.
>
>   **Example**: to jog slowly          scurry     lunge     sprint     <u>trot</u>

6.   covered by water          afloat     submerged     moist     buried

7.   a large amount            abundance     figure     remainder     addition

8.   active at night           restless     nocturnal     lethargic     energetic

9.   to scrape the skin        grind     grate     pamper     graze

10.  lacking strength          obscure     feeble     timid     slender

Select the most appropriate word from the table to complete each pair of antonyms below. Write the word on the corresponding line.

| qualified | necessary | adaptable | final | dismayed |
|---|---|---|---|---|
| disagreeable | wither | original | turmoil | undermine |

11. support        _____

12. unskilled      _____

13. inflexible     _____

14. flourish       _____

15. pleasant       _____

16. tranquillity   _____

17. fake           _____

18. delighted      _____

19. introductory   _____

20. needless       _____

Complete the word on the right so that it is a synonym, or nearly a synonym, of the word on the left.

**Example:**   rug        _car_ pet

21. launch         init_____e

22. pause          he_____ate

23. watch          mo_____or

24. excursion      ex_____ition

25. plod           t_____ge

**END OF TEST**

/ 25

© CGP — not to be photocopied

19

You have **10 minutes** to do this test.  Work as quickly and as accurately as you can.

> Find the word that is a synonym, or nearly a synonym, of the word on the left.
>
> **Example**: **wide**    flat    straight    <u>broad</u>    long

1. **greedy**        clenching    grasping    unthinking    heedless

2. **tend**          nurse    admire    glorify    charge

3. **capability**    cunning    sophistication    strength    competence

4. **still**         settling    powerless    senseless    motionless

5. **regularly**     routinely    orderly    fitfully    occasionally

6. **triumph**       compliment    honour    win    flatten

> Three of the words in each list are linked.  Mark the word that is not related to these three.
>
> **Example**: teacher    doctor    <u>hospital</u>    firefighter

7. windscreen    tyre    driveway    boot

8. terrifying    frightening    risky    alarming

9. suspend    proceed    progress    advance

10. drums    horn    cymbals    orchestra

11. coach    referee    reporter    footballer

12. shingle    shell    grit    gravel

© CGP — not to be photocopied

Underline the word that is the best antonym for the word in bold and makes sense in the sentence.

**Example:** Peter found the visit **dull**.    <u>exciting</u>  dreary  upsetting  boring

13. Violet's speech was very **coherent**.
    unclear   logical   vocal   unvaried

14. The workers completed their tasks **thoroughly**.
    foolishly   intelligently   carelessly   thoughtfully

15. The stone circle was an **insignificant** historical site.
    ancient   impermanent   mundane   important

16. The criminals stole a **forged** masterpiece.
    counterfeit   genuine   inauthentic   absolute

17. Jared **exaggerated** the extent of Maddie's misbehaviour.
    downplayed   announced   confessed   revealed

18. All the information in Siti's article was **accurate**.
    unhelpful   informative   incorrect   unusual

Mark the word outside the brackets that has a similar meaning to the words in both sets of brackets.

**Example:** (find discover) (stain blemish)    freckle  smudge  <u>spot</u>  see

19. (gleam  glow)      (scour  polish)        scrub  cleanse  shine  sparkle

20. (rubble  debris)   (stays  lingers)       waits  ruins  razes  remains

21. (grasp  grab)        (fragment  snippet)      seize  fleck  smidgen  snatch

22. (job  profession)    (run  rush)              career  occupation  course  track

23. (raft  buoy)         (drift  glide)           hover  bob  hang  float

24. (strip  clear)       (deserted  unoccupied)   unload  devoid  unfilled  empty

25. (disappear  fade)    (hand  give)             reach  throw  pass  vanish

**END OF TEST**

/ 25

# Puzzles 3

Puzzle time! This puzzle will help with your **word-knowledge** and **word-making** skills.

## Odds and Ends

In each of the houses below there is one word that isn't related to the other three. In each house, circle the odd word out. Then, pair up the twelve words you've circled to make six new words. You can only use each circled word once.

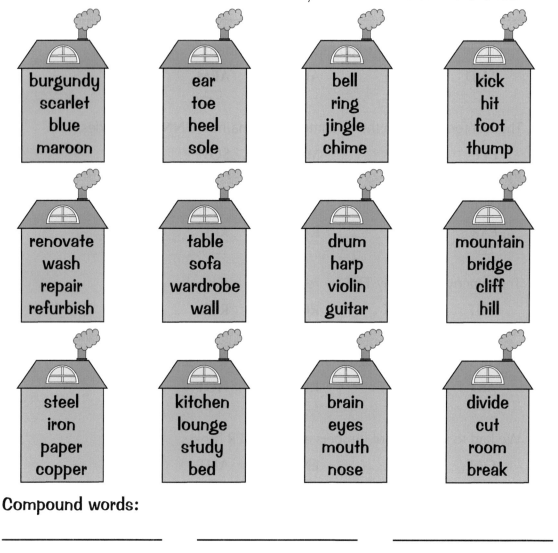

**Compound words:**

_____    _____    _____

_____    _____    _____

You have **10 minutes** to do this test.  Work as quickly and as accurately as you can.

Choose the correct three-letter word to complete the word in capital letters, so that it finishes the sentence in a sensible way.

**Example**:  It can be **CHY** outside when it snows.

| APP | ILL | EEK | ERR |
|:---:|:---:|:---:|:---:|
| ☐ | ▬ | ☐ | ☐ |

1.  Thankfully, nobody was **HED** in the car accident.

| AND | APE | AIL | ARM |
|:---:|:---:|:---:|:---:|
| ☐ | ☐ | ☐ | ☐ |

2.  The lost footage from the documentary remained **UNN** for decades.

| EVE | SEE | MOW | SOW |
|:---:|:---:|:---:|:---:|
| ☐ | ☐ | ☐ | ☐ |

3.  The contestant was disqualified for **BING** the judges.

| EAR | ALL | RAY | RIB |
|:---:|:---:|:---:|:---:|
| ☐ | ☐ | ☐ | ☐ |

4.  They uncovered many **THS** by reading the old book.

| RUT | INK | ROW | ROB |
|:---:|:---:|:---:|:---:|
| ☐ | ☐ | ☐ | ☐ |

5.  Simon saw the crab **STLE** behind a rock on the beach.

| ART | CUT | KIT | HUT |
|:---:|:---:|:---:|:---:|
| ☐ | ☐ | ☐ | ☐ |

6.  We had to wear lots of jumpers after the **BER** broke.

| OAT | OIL | END | ANT |
|:---:|:---:|:---:|:---:|
| ☐ | ☐ | ☐ | ☐ |

Look at the word on the left. Underline the category that it belongs to.

**Example**: scarlet        <u>red</u>    yellow    blue    green

7. sheep        meadow    farmer    livestock    wool

8. queen        emperor    ruler    state    palace

9. chisel        hammer    gadget    builder    tool

10. trainers        exercise    running    athletics    shoes

11. willow        orchard    tree    leaves    carpenter

12. heart        organ    kindness    blood    body

13. suitcase        backpack    package    luggage    clothing

Complete the word on the right so that it is an antonym, or nearly an antonym, of the word on the left.

**Example**: smooth   r o u g h

14. intentional   ☐ c c i ☐ ☐ n t ☐ ☐

15. moderation   ☐ x ☐ e s ☐

16. horizontal   v ☐ r t ☐ c ☐ ☐

17. insult   ☐ l a ☐ t ☐ r

18. increase   ☐ w ☐ n d ☐ e

19. conform   r ☐ b ☐ ☐

Find the word that is a synonym, or nearly a synonym, of the word on the left.

**Example**: **wide**    flat    straight    <u>broad</u>    long

20. **edible**        poisonous    eatable    unbelievable    sweet

21. **stubborn**      understanding    adamant    consumed    anguished

22. **suitable**      fitting    flexible    stylish    overstated

23. **substitute**    escalate    exchange    supply    rearrange

24. **revamp**        recite    improve    apply    worsen

25. **upkeep**        memento    maintenance    fund    property

**END OF TEST**

/ 25

© CGP — not to be photocopied

You have **10 minutes** to do this test.  Work as quickly and as accurately as you can.

> Underline the correct homophone to complete the sentence.
>
> **Example**: Archie tied a _____ in the ship's rigging.    not   <u>knot</u>

1.  The farmer can _____ thirty sheep in an hour.    shear   sheer

2.  The child was disappointed and started to _____.    whine   wine

3.  Some archeologists found an ancient Greek _____.    earn   urn

4.  The local _____ is building a new road.    counsel   council

5.  The pirates plan to attack the ship and _____ it.    loot   lute

6.  Sami and Kamil rowed along the winding _____.    creek   creak

> Look at the definition on the left.  Underline the word on the right that best matches the definition.
>
> **Example**: to jog slowly        scurry    lunge    sprint    <u>trot</u>

7.  to set on fire        stove    expire    ignite    alight

8.  to dig out        collapse    excavate    irrigate    enrage

9.  a strange thing        peculiarity    quality    manner    whim

10. self-obsessed        forbidding    selfless    conceited    polite

11. to jerk suddenly        twinge    wobble    twitch    pounce

12. to vote someone in        curb    elect    withhold    allocate

Complete the word on the right so that it is a synonym, or nearly a synonym, of the word on the left.

**Example**: rug     _car_ pet

13. scowl                    _____mace

14. truthful            fai_____l

15. unsympathetic    hea_____ss

16. plucky              cou_____ous

17. shake               vib_____e

18. resist                    _____stand

19. warrant            per_____

Underline the word that is the best antonym for the word in bold and makes sense in the sentence.

**Example**: Peter found the visit **dull**.     <u>exciting</u>  dreary  upsetting  boring

20. Only one of the toilet cubicles was **vacant**.

    occupied   committed   devoured   detested

21. Simona was **undecided** about what colour the walls should be.

    thwarted   indecisive   certain   concerned

22. The general put the army on the **defensive**.

    exclusive   offensive   protection   aggression

23. Mowing the lawn can be a very **tedious** job.

    perplexing   exciting   frustrating   daunting

24. The seats on this flight feel very **spacious**.

    tight-fisted   confined   uncomfortable   roomy

25. The variety of food served at the **new** restaurant was disappointing.

    cultural   established   animated   contemporary

**END OF TEST**

/ 25

© CGP — not to be photocopied

# Test 10

You have **10 minutes** to do this test. Work as quickly and as accurately as you can.

Mark the word outside the brackets that has a similar meaning to the words in both sets of brackets.

**Example**: (find discover) (stain blemish)    freckle   smudge   <u>spot</u>   see

1.  (technique  way)    (drive  road)        form   system   street   approach

2.  (likelihood  odds) (opportunity  opening)   chance   risk   fortune   option

3.  (art  skill)        (ship  boat)        craft   job   prowess   cruise

4.  (distant  faraway)  (unlikely  improbable)   slim   unreliable   isolated   remote

5.  (turn  twirl)        (warp  distort)      coil   deform   buckle   twist

Underline a word from the first set, followed by a word from the second set, that go together to form a new word.

**Example**: (<u>water</u> suggest disc) (<u>fall</u> hard ton)   (The word is **waterfall**.)

6.  (shoe  note  home)        (off  wife  book)

7.  (any  dare  trick)        (treat  person  devil)

8.  (flower  grass  promise)    (sun  hopper  sing)

9.  (land  cave  up)        (make  in  slide)

10. (back  foot  in)        (sack  wear  cross)

Test 10          30          © CGP — not to be photocopied

Select the most appropriate word from the table to complete each pair of synonyms below. Write the word on the corresponding line.

| confusion | feasible | order | vigilant | implore |
|-----------|----------|-------|----------|---------|
| booming | modernise | possibly | utterly | grieve |

11. completely _____

12. possible _____

13. mourn _____

14. tidiness _____

15. alert _____

16. successful _____

17. potentially _____

18. update _____

19. disarray _____

20. beg _____

Complete the word on the right so that it is an antonym, or nearly an antonym, of the word on the left.

**Example:** smooth     r _oug_ h

21. satisfy        disa_____nt

22. fortify        we_____n

23. tactless       tho_____ful

24. united         d_____ded

25. foreground     _____ground

**END OF TEST**

/ 25

Break time!  These puzzles are great for practising your **word-making** and **sentence** skills.

# The Pirate's Code

Solve the coded message below to find out where the treasure is hidden.

Start with the shortest word.  Using the letters provided, work out what the most likely missing letter could be.  Once you think you've worked it out, check to see whether you can add that letter anywhere else.  Then add it to the grid, and move on to another number.

You'll have to use your knowledge of word formation along with a bit of trial and error to solve the puzzle!

*The letters marked with an 'X' don't appear in the puzzle.*

|     | N   |     | E   |     |   | T   |     | E   |   |     |     |     |     | N   | T   |
| --- | --- | --- | --- | --- | - | --- | --- | --- | - | --- | --- | --- | --- | --- | --- |
| 3   | 17  | 12  | 7   | 21  |   | 4   | 19  | 7   |   | 1   | 23  | 1   | 23  | 17  | 3   | 4 |

|     | T   |     | E   | E   |   |     |     | T   |     |   | E   |     |     |     | T   |
| --- | --- | --- | --- | --- | - | --- | --- | --- | --- | - | --- | --- | --- | --- | --- |
| 4   | 21  | 7   | 7   |     |   | 13  | 8   | 4   | 19  |   | 7   | 8   | 14  | 19  | 4 |

|     | E   |     | V   | E   |     |
| --- | --- | --- | --- | --- | --- |
| 5   | 7   | 10  | 26  | 7   | 20  |

| A | B | C | D | E | F | G | H | I | J | K | L | M | N  | O | P | Q | R | S | T | U | V  | W | X | Y | Z |
|---|---|---|---|---|---|---|---|---|---|---|---|---|----|---|---|---|---|---|---|---|----|---|---|---|---|
|   | X |   |   | 7 | X |   |   |   | X | X |   | X | 17 | X | X |   |   |   | 4 |   | 26 |   | X | X | X |

# Lose a Letter

Remove one letter from each word in bold to make a new word that makes sense at the end of the sentence.

On her **break**, Sandra saw a bird with a worm in its _____.

The woman with **brown** hair wiped the sweat from her _____.

Although she was once a **friend**, Riyad felt Jess was now a _____.

**10**

You have **10 minutes** to do this test.  Work as quickly and as accurately as you can.

Underline the correct homophone to complete the sentence.

**Example**: Archie tied a _____ in the ship's rigging.     not   <u>knot</u>

1.   Buffaloes used to roam this _____.                       plain   plane

2.   The water at the _____ had gotten higher.          quay   key

3.   Jasmine wants to _____ her own house.               build   billed

4.   Beth measured the _____ of the flour.                wait   weight

5.   The boat battled the strong _____.                     current   currant

6.   The park was a great _____ for a picnic.            plaice   place

Mark the word outside the brackets that has a similar meaning to the words in both sets of brackets.

**Example**: (find  discover) (stain  blemish)     freckle  smudge  <u>spot</u>  see

7.   (mistake  blunder)   (slink  sneak)          trip  slip  move  dive

8.   (kind  gentle)          (tending  minding)     caring  tender  nice  helping

9.   (nip  tweak)            (dash  drop)             tweeze  grip  pinch  hurt

10. (sequence  series)   (pedal  bicycle)       movement  structure  ride  cycle

11. (agreement  pact)   (deal  haggle)           bargain  price  handle  swap

12. (appear  sprout)     (multiply  expand)     boost  grow  flower  shoot

Find the word that is an antonym, or nearly an antonym, of the word on the left.

**Example**: **first**   later   <u>last</u>   next   beginning

13. **rarely**        averagely   frequently   moderately   mundanely

14. **disprove**      think   guess   approve   validate

15. **careful**       neglectful   sly   thoughtful   ruthless

16. **able**          adequate   inelegant   incapable   impractical

17. **warmth**        heat   frostiness   glacier   freezer

18. **memorable**     sloppy   forgetful   notable   forgettable

19. **easygoing**     strict   tolerant   accepting   spiteful

Underline the word that is the best synonym for the word in bold and makes sense in the sentence.

**Example**: The river was **broad**.   flowing   muddy   <u>wide</u>   fast

20. Dylan thought that the questions were **bewildering**.
    hasty   puzzling   upsetting   hilarious

21. The food looked so **appetising** that Chiara's stomach rumbled.
    intricate   enormous   tempting   delicate

22. Isobel's dad said some fresh air would **cure** her headache.
    relieve   enhance   delete   excuse

23. I am preparing for a **strenuous** cross-country race.

recognised    rugged    scenic    punishing

24. Juan's mum says that he has a real **keenness** for life.

unease    acceptance    zest    tolerance

25. Milly's brand new football boots were **untarnished**.

unblemished    expensive    glossy    unfashionable

**END OF TEST**

/ 25

(10)

You have **10 minutes** to do this test. Work as quickly and as accurately as you can.

Choose the correct three-letter word to complete the word in capital letters, so that it finishes the sentence in a sensible way.

**Example**: It can be **CHY** outside when it snows.

| APP | ILL | EEK | ERR |
|-----|-----|-----|-----|
| ☐ | ▬ | ☐ | ☐ |

1. He was **DING** a blanket over the baby just as it started to rain.

| AMP | ART | ASH | RAP |
|-----|-----|-----|-----|
| ☐ | ☐ | ☐ | ☐ |

2. I am **WING** the mud out of my clothes.

| ARM | ANT | ILL | ASH |
|-----|-----|-----|-----|
| ☐ | ☐ | ☐ | ☐ |

3. Nicki climbed the **LER** to get into the treehouse.

| ADD | OAF | APE | END |
|-----|-----|-----|-----|
| ☐ | ☐ | ☐ | ☐ |

4. Ming wants to have a **CER** as an astronaut.

| AMP | RAT | ARE | OLD |
|-----|-----|-----|-----|
| ☐ | ☐ | ☐ | ☐ |

5. The tiger **PLS** through the thick jungle.

| ACE | EAR | EAT | ROW |
|-----|-----|-----|-----|
| ☐ | ☐ | ☐ | ☐ |

Select the most appropriate word from the table to complete each pair of antonyms below. Write the word on the corresponding line.

| reduction | collected | carefully | slightly | rough |
|-----------|-----------|-----------|----------|-------|
| fresh | favourite | moisten | heighten | disagree |

6.  clumsily _____

7.  musty _____

8.  sleek _____

9.  underdog _____

10. extremely _____

11. panicky _____

12. dampen _____

13. dry _____

14. consent _____

15. enlargement _____

Complete the word on the right so that it is a synonym, or nearly a synonym, of the word on the left.

**Example:** rug ___car_pet

16. envious           je_____s

17. glimmer           fl_____er

18. handbook          _____ual

19. unsuspecting      unk_____g

20. march             pa_____de

Look at the word on the left. Underline the category that it belongs to.

**Example**: scarlet      <u>red</u>    yellow    blue    green

21. watercolour      performance    painting    beverage    shade

22. mile      distance    speed    volume    weight

23. wheat      agriculture    harvester    cotton    cereal

24. strudel      recipe    cooking    dessert    sugar

25. helicopter      aircraft    airlift    propellor    rescue

**END OF TEST**

/ 25

You have **10 minutes** to do this test. Work as quickly and as accurately as you can.

Complete the word on the right so that it is an antonym, or nearly an antonym, of the word on the left.

**Example**: smooth | r | o | u | g | h |

1. fondness    | | i | s | | i | k | |

2. undependable    | r | e | | i | a | | l | |

3. early    | | e | l | | t | | d |

4. merciless    | | o | | g | | v | | n | g |

5. dither    | d | | c | | | e |

6. uncontrolled    | d | | s | c | | p | l | | | e | d |

7. focussed    | | i | | t | | a | c | | e | d |

Three of the words in each list are linked. Mark the word that is not related to these three.

**Example**: teacher   doctor   <u>hospital</u>   firefighter

8. stroll   amble   bolt   meander

9. overcast   cloudy   foggy   fine

10. penguin   reindeer   robin   turkey

11. traveller   wanderer   settler   rover

12. velvet   soft   silk   linen

13. consider   ponder   complete   meditate

---

Underline the word that is the best synonym for the word in bold and makes sense in the sentence.

**Example**: The river was **broad**.   flowing   muddy   <u>wide</u>   fast

14. The writing in the diary was **unreadable**.
    neat   illegible   elaborate   intriguing

15. Farzana loved **frolicking** in the snow.
    playing   hiding   cheering   walking

16. Mark got into trouble for **tampering** with the fire alarm.
    repairing   breaking   meddling   arguing

17. Flo was completely **unaware** of what was happening.
    indifferent   ignorant   conscious   carefree

18. The explorer had been **longing** to see the world.
    measuring   yearning   aiming   trying

19. The plans to build a petting zoo in the school aren't **workable**.
    sociable   developed   convenient   viable

                         © CGP — not to be photocopied

Look at the definition on the left.  Underline the word on the right that best matches the definition.

**Example**: to jog slowly        scurry    lunge    sprint    <u>trot</u>

20. having no skill        awkward   upset   troubled   inept

21. to put up with        insist   endure   encounter   instruct

22. to say again        describe   report   reiterate   reply

23. an ongoing fight        accord   feud   hating   frustration

24. as good as new        pure   untidy   luxurious   pristine

25. lively and noisy        boisterous   placid   drowsy   fiery

**END OF TEST**

/ 25

# Puzzles 5

Break time!  These puzzles are a great way to practise your **word-making** and **logic** skills.

## The Great Escape

Two spies have entered a villain's lair and uncovered their evil plan, but they now need to get to the escape point without being spotted.

There are two safe routes to the exit.  Each one spells out a six-letter word that means **evil**.  For each word, draw a line from the start to the escape point to connect the letters of the word together.  Each circle can only be used once. The first connection has been made for you.

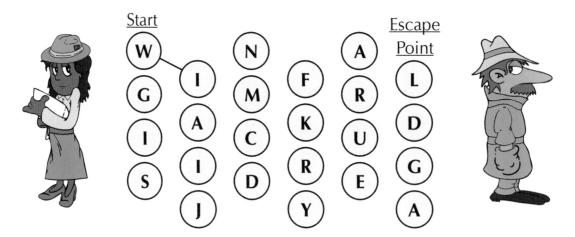

## Riddle Me This

Can you solve this riddle?  Write your answer on the line below.

I fly but I have no wings.

I pass but I play no games.

I am endless, yet people say I'm so short.

What am I?

Answer to the riddle: _____

42

© CGP — not to be photocopied

You have **10 minutes** to do this test.  Work as quickly and as accurately as you can.

Choose the correct three-letter word to complete the word in capital letters, so that it finishes the sentence in a sensible way.

**Example**:  It can be **CHY** outside when it snows.

| APP | ILL | EEK | ERR |
|-----|-----|-----|-----|
| ☐ | ▬ | ☐ | ☐ |

1. I spent all day **TING** to the plants in the garden.

| ASK | END | OIL | AIL |
|-----|-----|-----|-----|
| ☐ | ☐ | ☐ | ☐ |

2. The firefighters **REED** immediately when they got the emergency call.

| LAY | MIX | ACT | FIX |
|-----|-----|-----|-----|
| ☐ | ☐ | ☐ | ☐ |

3. Everyone was walking very **SLY** because the roads were icy.

| OWL | TEE | PRY | IMP |
|-----|-----|-----|-----|
| ☐ | ☐ | ☐ | ☐ |

4. The boat **FLED** away when I let go of the rope.

| ASH | OAT | APP | OUT |
|-----|-----|-----|-----|
| ☐ | ☐ | ☐ | ☐ |

5. Newton said some **UND** things to Anwar.

| TIE | WIN | USE | KIN |
|-----|-----|-----|-----|
| ☐ | ☐ | ☐ | ☐ |

6. Nia and Adam **DEED** their run until after it stopped raining.

| FIN | BAT | LAY | SIR |
|-----|-----|-----|-----|
| ☐ | ☐ | ☐ | ☐ |

Find the word that is an antonym, or nearly an antonym, of the word on the left.

**Example**: **first**   later  <u>last</u>  next  beginning

7. **orderly**     distributed  baffled  disorganised  uncluttered

8. **restless**     calm  shaken  fatigued  weary

9. **doubtful**     excited  confident  brash  cheeky

10. **bold**     cowardly  brazen  worthless  sickly

11. **normal**     regular  peculiar  unplanned  changeable

12. **assistance**     concealment  disagreement  improvement  hindrance

Underline a word from the first set, followed by a word from the second set, that go together to form a new word.

**Example**: (<u>water</u> suggest disc) (<u>fall</u> hard ton)  (The word is **waterfall**.)

13. (hide  rot  night)     (rate  hood  ten)

14. (bar  ball  bull)     (burr  gain  let)

15. (ear  ice  sleep)     (wax  call  sing)

16. (me  see  off)     (all  eyes  end)

17. (no  or  every)     (deal  won  kid)

18. (flag  bit  can)     (pole  door  vent)

          © CGP — not to be photocopied

Complete the word on the right so that it is a synonym, or nearly a synonym, of the word on the left.

**Example**: rug  [c] [a] [r] [p] [e] [t]

19. bleak  [d] [r] [ ] [a] [r] [ ]

20. presume  [ ] [u] [ ] [p] [ ] [s] [e]

21. miraculous  [a] [ ] [ ] [z] [ ] [n] [g]

22. level-headed  [s] [ ] [n] [ ] [i] [b] [ ] [e]

23. redo  [r] [ ] [p] [ ] [ ] [t]

24. find  [ ] [o] [ ] [a] [t] [ ]

25. equal  [m] [ ] [ ] [c] [h]

**END OF TEST**

/ 25

© CGP — not to be photocopied

Test 14

You have **10 minutes** to do this test.  Work as quickly and as accurately as you can.

> Find the word that is a synonym, or nearly a synonym, of the word on the left.
>
> **Example**: **wide**   flat   straight   <u>broad</u>   long

1.  **allow**        enable   advise   prevent   unchain

2.  **dribble**      weep   gush   pour   trickle

3.  **harm**         overwhelm   demolish   injure   exhaust

4.  **willpower**    readiness   determination   easiness   necessity

5.  **useful**       preferable   worthwhile   rewarding   active

6.  **constant**     relenting   tiring   opinionated   persistent

> Three of the words in each list are linked.  Mark the word that is not related to these three.
>
> **Example**: teacher   doctor   <u>hospital</u>   firefighter

7.  draw   goal   tie   lose

8.  lettuce   broccoli   moss   spinach

9.  diagram   drawing   designer   picture

10. occasion   celebration   event   grouping

11. loot   kidnap   steal   plunder

12. supplier   shopper   customer   buyer

Look at the word on the left. Underline the category that it belongs to.

Example: scarlet          <u>red</u>     yellow     blue     green

13. drawbridge          screen     castle     history     defence

14. wax          substance     fabric     candle     light

15. Europe          city     county     nation     continent

16. toll          road     money     fee     coin

17. winter          month     weather     temperature     season

18. prank          game     pastime     trick     hobby

---

Complete the word on the right so that it is a synonym, or nearly a synonym, of the word on the left.

Example: rug  c a r p e t

19. rare          s c ☐ r c ☐

20. eagerness          e ☐ t h u ☐ ☐ a s ☐

21. environment          h ☐ b i ☐ ☐ t

22. better          ☐ u p e ☐ i ☐ r

23. drive      [s] [t] [ ] [ ] [r]

24. journey      [ ] [o] [y] [a] [ ] [ ]

25. adventurous      [d] [a] [ ] [i] [ ] [ ]

**END OF TEST**

[    / 25 ]

# Test 16

You have **10 minutes** to do this test. Work as quickly and as accurately as you can.

> Look at the definition on the left. Underline the word on the right that best matches the definition.
>
> **Example**: to jog slowly     scurry    lunge    sprint    <u>trot</u>

1. a little island     coast    islet    shore    snorkel

2. to join in     participate    clasp    affix    share

3. to admire a lot     compromise    idolise    bless    hail

4. weak and cowardly     boneless    headless    hapless    spineless

5. an extravagant meal     brunch    supper    banquet    treat

6. to find out     situate    design    explore    discover

> Underline a word from the first set, followed by a word from the second set, that go together to form a new word.
>
> **Example**: (<u>water</u> suggest disc) (<u>fall</u> hard ton)    (The word is **waterfall**.)

7. (head play win)    (jump hit list)

8. (draw fear awe)    (sum back red)

9. (hand more few)    (under made go)

10. (hope gull bear)    (able full rings)

11. (come fore hell)    (met see ward)

12. (up get switch)    (drop on out)

Complete the word on the right so that it is an antonym, or nearly an antonym, of the word on the left.

**Example**: smooth      r _oug_ h

13. toil                 r_____t

14. ajar                clo_____

15. ashamed       sha_____ss

16. insecurity      sta_____y

17. shakily         ste_____y

18. complicate     si_____ify

19. fail                su_____d

Underline the word that is the best antonym for the word in bold and makes sense in the sentence.

**Example**: Peter found the visit **dull**.    <u>exciting</u>  dreary  upsetting  boring

20. Clementine felt **exhausted** after playing hockey.
    peckish   cheerless   irritated   invigorated

21. Jessica couldn't hide her **satisfaction** after the football team won.
    relief   boredom   displeasure   excitement

22. During the tournament, Shakti became **fascinated** by netball.
    bored   dazzled   untroubled   riveted

 © CGP — not to be photocopied

23. Lars dressed **formally** for the party.

    dramatically    casually    determinedly    sincerely

24. Tifa tries to do **gentle** exercise at least twice a week.

    fit    severe    rigorous    expiring

25. When the third book in the series came out, I read it **slowly**.

    rapidly    eventually    deliberately    gleefully

**END OF TEST**

/ 25

Time for a break!  These puzzles are a great way to practise your **word-making** skills.

# Homophone Hunt

Unscramble the letters below to make words that match the definitions.

dressing for food
e s u a c
➡ _ _ _ _ _

place after third
t o h f r u
➡ _ _ _ _ _ _

a solemn pledge
c a p t
➡ _ _ _ _

interfere
d l e e m d
➡ _ _ _ _ _ _

a smell
e t n s c
➡ _ _ _ _ _

there are seven in a week
d y a s
➡ _ _ _ _

Now write out the homophone of each of the unscrambled words on the lines below.  Then find each of these new words in the wordsearch.

_____

_____

_____

_____

_____

_____

| s | d | u | g | u | e | s | e |
|---|---|---|---|---|---|---|---|
| o | e | c | r | u | o | s | z |
| a | k | t | a | l | z | e | a |
| r | c | h | d | z | a | g | d |
| l | a | d | e | m | e | s | s |
| c | p | r | p | k | d | e | o |
| e | o | r | a | c | e | n | z |
| f | f | o | r | t | h | t | t |

You have **10 minutes** to do this test.  Work as quickly and as accurately as you can.

> Underline the correct homophone to complete the sentence.
>
> **Example**: Archie tied a _____ in the ship's rigging.    not   <u>knot</u>

1.  Zhao read his book _____.                              aloud   allowed

2.  Sam's dad had chocolate _____ for dessert.            moose   mousse

3.  The bin started to _____ after a week.                reek   wreak

4.  Krista's friend criticised her for being _____.       vein   vain

5.  Marge _____ the secret out of her sister.             pried   pride

> Mark the word outside the brackets that has a similar meaning to the words in both sets of brackets.
>
> **Example**: (find  discover) (stain  blemish)      freckle   smudge   <u>spot</u>   see

6.  (past  after)        (exceeding  above)      surpass  beyond  next  outshine

7.  (support  back)      (victor  winner)        champion  fan  patron  value

8.  (flee  bolt)         (avoid  evade)          run  escape  fly  miss

9.  (stubby  small)      (flying  fleeting)      abrupt  short  gliding  petite

10. (crouch  hunch)      (stocky  stumpy)        perch  duck  squat  sturdy

© CGP — not to be photocopied

Select the most appropriate word from the table to complete each pair of antonyms below. Write the word on the corresponding line.

| conquered | lose | hatred | tame | thoughtless |
|---|---|---|---|---|
| truth | lengthen | demotivated | modern | demote |

11. ferocious  _____

12. acquire  _____

13. liberated  _____

14. promote  _____

15. love  _____

16. considerate  _____

17. outdated  _____

18. energised  _____

19. fiction  _____

20. condense  _____

Complete the word on the right so that it is a synonym, or nearly a synonym, of the word on the left.

**Example**: rug  [c][a][r][p][e][t]

21. advantage  [b][ ][n][ ][f][ ][ ]

22. offer  [v][o][ ][u][n][ ][e][ ][r]

23. horrifying  [c][ ][i][l][ ][ ][n][ ]

24. border  [ ][ ][r][g][ ][n]

25. protective  [d][ ][f][ ][n][ ][ ][v][e]

**END OF TEST**

/ 25

Test 17                    54                    © CGP — not to be photocopied

You have **10 minutes** to do this test.  Work as quickly and as accurately as you can.

Choose the correct three-letter word to complete the word in capital letters, so that it finishes the sentence in a sensible way.

**Example**:  It can be **CHY** outside when it snows.

|  APP  |  ILL  |  EEK  |  ERR  |
|:-----:|:-----:|:-----:|:-----:|
| ☐ | ▬ | ☐ | ☐ |

1. The cheese knife was on the kitchen counter next to the **GER**.

|  LID  |  RAT  |  ROW  |  AND  |
|:-----:|:-----:|:-----:|:-----:|
| ☐ | ☐ | ☐ | ☐ |

2. My grandma is **WING** a purple cardigan underneath her coat.

|  EAR  |  ADD  |  AIL  |  AFT  |
|:-----:|:-----:|:-----:|:-----:|
| ☐ | ☐ | ☐ | ☐ |

3. Alex had been dancing since he was an **INT**.

|  CAN  |  FAN  |  TEN  |  DEN  |
|:-----:|:-----:|:-----:|:-----:|
| ☐ | ☐ | ☐ | ☐ |

4. Chidi bought Elinor flowers to make **ADS** for his actions.

|  WAR  |  MEN  |  OPT  |  ORE  |
|:-----:|:-----:|:-----:|:-----:|
| ☐ | ☐ | ☐ | ☐ |

5. We searched the fridge to find the **SCE** of the strange smell.

|  CAR  |  TAN  |  HEM  |  OUR  |
|:-----:|:-----:|:-----:|:-----:|
| ☐ | ☐ | ☐ | ☐ |

6. They **REE** the classic film with new actors.

|  FIN  |  SUM  |  MAD  |  PUT  |
|:-----:|:-----:|:-----:|:-----:|
| ☐ | ☐ | ☐ | ☐ |

© CGP — not to be photocopied

Three of the words in each list are linked. Mark the word
that is not related to these three.

**Example**: teacher   doctor   <u>hospital</u>   firefighter

7.   tomato   celery   cucumber   potato

8.   analyse   research   muse   probe

9.   kangaroo   mule   stallion   donkey

10.  left   departed   detached   went

11.  restrict   adjust   confine   limit

12.  episode   chapter   cinema   scene

Complete the word on the right so that it is an antonym,
or nearly an antonym, of the word on the left.

**Example**: smooth        r <u>oug</u> h

13.  growth          dec_____e

14.  tiny            m_____ve

15.  bend            st_____hten

16.  adoration       l_____hing

17.  polluted        c_____n

18.  remove          repl_____

19.  unashamed       em_____ssed

Find the word that is a synonym, or nearly a synonym, of the word on the left.

**Example**: **wide**    flat    straight    <u>broad</u>    long

20. **agile**       nimble    accelerated    stealthy    coordinated

21. **poison**      antidote    toxin    complaint    attack

22. **booked**      offered    socialised    reserved    worked

23. **robber**      villain    bandit    agent    beggar

24. **tremble**     waver    flail    frighten    rotate

25. **fight**       surrender    challenge    strike    skirmish

**END OF TEST**

/ 25

You have **10 minutes** to do this test.  Work as quickly and as accurately as you can.

> Complete the word on the right so that it is an antonym,
> or nearly an antonym, of the word on the left.
>
> **Example**: smooth  r o u g h

1.  soften     t ☐ ☐ g ☐ ☐ n

2.  level     s ☐ a ☐ t ☐ d

3.  slight     l ☐ r g ☐

4.  unbind     r ☐ ☐ t ☐ a i n

5.  affectionate     u ☐ l o ☐ ☐ n ☐

> Mark the word outside the brackets that has a similar meaning to the words in
> both sets of brackets.
>
> **Example**: (find discover) (stain blemish)     freckle  smudge  <u>spot</u>  see

6.  (mark  stain)     (dab  pat)     damage  splash  blot  hit

7.  (trail  footway)     (route  way)     line  path  direction  lane

8.  (plug  seal)     (load  pack)     throng  overfill  clog  fill

9.  (hamper  inhibit)     (feat  trick)     bizarre  stunt  hinder  antic

10. (pleat  crease)     (envelop  wrap)     fold  flounder  crinkle  curl

Look at the definition on the left. Underline the word on the right that best matches the definition.

**Example**: to jog slowly      scurry    lunge    sprint    <u>trot</u>

11. to say sorry      block    apologise    regret    underachieve

12. easily broken      damaging    breakable    crisp    strapping

13. a member of a country      citizen    tourist    participant    official

14. to drive forward      connect    rebound    commute    propel

15. things crashing together      collision    shock    fragmentation    topple

Select the most appropriate word from the table to complete each pair of synonyms below. Write the word on the corresponding line.

| atrocious | imitate | genius | ravenous | object |
|-----------|---------|--------|----------|--------|
| evacuate | catastrophe | union | supervise | dwelling |

16. mimic     _____

17. oversee     _____

18. horrible     _____

19. alliance     _____

20. residence     _____

21. hungry     _____

22. tragedy     _____

23. oppose     _____

24. leave     _____

25. mastermind     _____

**END OF TEST**

/ 25

Time for another puzzle! This puzzle is great for practising your **word-knowledge** skills.

# The Jumbled Sea

Unscramble the anagrams below to get the names of different animals that live in or near water. Then fill in the grid below with the unscrambled animals.

**LASE**

**BARC**

**KRASH**

**LEWAH**

**TETRUL**

**HOLDPIN**

**AESGLUL**

**SHIGDOLF**

**CRILODOCE**

*If you're struggling to get the word, try rearranging the letters in a different order.*

60

© CGP — not to be photocopied

You have **10 minutes** to do this test. Work as quickly and as accurately as you can.

> Find the word that is an antonym, or nearly an antonym, of the word on the left.
>
> **Example**: **first**    later    <u>last</u>    next    beginning

1. **admission**    expulsion   involvement   removal   secrecy

2. **merge**    separate   reattach   destroy   connect

3. **ungrateful**    appreciative   thankless   neighbourly   modest

4. **disliked**    friendly   unwanted   popular   haughty

5. **aggressive**    peaceable   fierce   arrogant   boastful

6. **numerous**    various   few   innumerable   countless

> Underline the correct homophone to complete the sentence.
>
> **Example**: Archie tied a _____ in the ship's rigging.    not   <u>knot</u>

7. We have more female rabbits than _____ ones.    male   mail

8. The _____ poured out of the volcano.    lava   larva

9. The _____ gave commands to his troops.    kernel   colonel

10. Annie felt very _____ after the marathon.    feint   faint

11. Mr Jenkins _____ his heavy bag around.    hauls   halls

12. Robert has _____ when it comes to fashion.    style   stile

Complete the word on the right so that it is a synonym,
or nearly a synonym, of the word on the left.

**Example**:   rug        _car_ pet

13.  immoral        e_____l

14.  inflate         sw_____

15.  sorrowful      _____ppy

16.  amass          g_____her

17.  excellent       outs_____ing

18.  provisions     s_____lies

19.  urge           en_____age

Choose the correct three-letter word to complete the word in capital letters,
so that it finishes the sentence in a sensible way.

**Example**:  It can be **CHY** outside when it snows.

| APP | ILL | EEK | ERR |
|-----|-----|-----|-----|
| ☐ | ■ | ☐ | ☐ |

20.  My sister found a **CHING** little cottage in the village.

| ARM | ART | ANT | AIR |
|-----|-----|-----|-----|
| ☐ | ☐ | ☐ | ☐ |

21.  Thando always **SCS** her friends with her spooky stories.

| ARE | OFF | ORE | OLD |
|-----|-----|-----|-----|
| ☐ | ☐ | ☐ | ☐ |

22. The knights wore **CLS** with the royal emblem on them.

**RAW** ☐   **AMP** ☐   **OWN** ☐   **OAK** ☐

23. The queen had several **THRS** built for her daughters.

**OAT** ☐   **ONE** ☐   **ILL** ☐   **EAT** ☐

24. A dictionary can help you **DEE** difficult words.

**LET** ☐   **BAT** ☐   **SIR** ☐   **FIN** ☐

25. They **STD** their bags in the luggage compartment.

**AGE** ☐   **ARE** ☐   **EWE** ☐   **OWE** ☐

**END OF TEST**

/ 25

You have **10 minutes** to do this test.  Work as quickly and as accurately as you can.

Find the word that is an antonym, or nearly an antonym, of the word on the left.

**Example**:  **first**    later    <u>last</u>    next    beginning

1.  **spirited**     lively    ghostly    lifeless    enthused

2.  **reassure**     explain    guarantee    unnerve    persuade

3.  **trust**     believe    doubt    dread    assume

4.  **buy**     stock    vend    swap    apportion

5.  **unknown**     vague    special    familiar    typical

6.  **lawful**     permitted    dubious    guilty    criminal

Complete the word on the right so that it is a synonym, or nearly a synonym, of the word on the left.

**Example**:  rug    c a r p e t

7.  incentive    ⬚ o t ⬚ v a ⬚ i ⬚ n

8.  scanty    s ⬚ a r s ⬚

9. village     s ☐ t t ☐ ☐ m e ☐ t

10. requirement     d ☐ m a ☐ d

11. instant     i ☐ ☐ e d ☐ ☐ t e

12. obstacle     ☐ a ☐ r ☐ e r

13. castle     f ☐ r t r ☐ ☐ s

---

Look at the word on the left.  Underline the category that it belongs to.

**Example**: scarlet       <u>red</u>    yellow    blue    green

14. goose     lake    waterbird    berry    chicken

15. parcel     post    stamp    letterbox    packaging

16. missile     gun    fuse    cannon    weapon

17. eclair     baker    cupcake    pastry    coffee

18. library     book    room    shop    writing

19. theft     offender    rob    crime    thief

Look at the definition on the left. Underline the word on the right that best matches the definition.

**Example**: to jog slowly       scurry    lunge    sprint    <u>trot</u>

20. someone who fights     crook    warrior    jester    knave

21. a place of safety     cottage    plaza    court    refuge

22. to strengthen     reinforce    assemble    saturate    mass

23. still and foul     erupting    dirty    stagnant    smooth

24. to be obsessed with     incensed    fixated    interested    disgusted

25. to want something     fulfil    desire    anticipate    misplace

**END OF TEST**

/ 25

⏱ 10

You have **10 minutes** to do this test.  Work as quickly and as accurately as you can.

Three of the words in each list are linked.  Mark the word that is not related to these three.

**Example**: teacher   doctor   <u>hospital</u>   firefighter

1.  buzz   hum   drone   fly

2.  fabrication   trickery   fib   falsehood

3.  doorway   entrance   corridor   gate

4.  trombone   conductor   trumpet   tuba

5.  pilot   wing   cockpit   engine

6.  outrage   awe   wrath   anger

Underline a word from the first set, followed by a word from the second set, that go together to form a new word.

**Example**: (<u>water</u> suggest disc) (<u>fall</u> hard ton)   (The word is **waterfall**.)

7.  (jack   brush   black)      (pan   pot   low)

8.  (jig   bowl   watch)      (life   see   tower)

9.  (hot   hand   back)      (some   mouth   post)

10. (desk   work   table)      (boy   spoon   art)

11. (park   stand   rest)      (still   store   hop)

12. (bone   wall   life)      (let   guard   knee)

© CGP — not to be photocopied                    67

Look at the word on the left. Underline the category that it belongs to.

**Example**: scarlet <u>red</u> yellow blue green

13. vandal      creator    <u>lawbreaker</u>    burglar    prisoner

14. recliner      hammock    swing    <u>furniture</u>    stool

15. cinnamon      odour    <u>spice</u>    dish    food

16. sculptor      <u>artist</u>    bust    painter    exhibition

17. laptop      electronic    <u>device</u>    connection    process

18. flask      china    crockery    tea    <u>container</u>

19. president      parliament    <u>leader</u>    general    king

Underline the word that is the best antonym for the word in bold and makes sense in the sentence.

**Example**: Peter found the visit **dull**.    <u>exciting</u> dreary upsetting boring

20. Ian is known for his **unenthusiastic** approach to playing chess.
zealous    passionless    strategic    measured

21. There is a **revolting** smell coming from the kitchen.
awful    delightful    strange    distressing

22. There was **harmony** in the kingdom after the banquet.
melody    discord    hesitancy    distraction

23. The country decided to **import** lots of pineapples this summer.

    transport    support    export    reimport

24. The **vast** garden is looked after very well by my sister.

    void    attractive    miniscule    cheap

25. The large foyer of the old mansion was **grandly** decorated.

    tidily    wildly    elegantly    modestly


**END OF TEST**

/ 25

It's puzzle time! This puzzle is a great way to practise your **vocabulary** skills.

# Marvellous Maps

There is some buried treasure somewhere on Infamous Isle. Each clue leads to a square on the map below. Once you've found it, jot down the coordinates. Then, unscramble the letters to reveal another clue for where the treasure is buried.

The first one has been done for you.

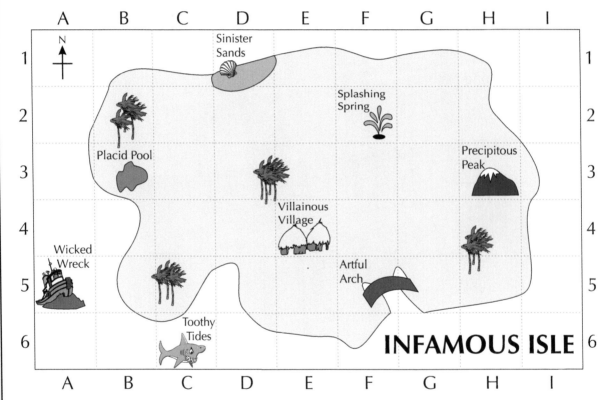

1. Nefarious dwellings: ( _E_ , _4_ )
2. Marooned mariners: ( __ , __ )
3. Steep mountain: ( __ , __ )

4. Still waters: ( __ , __ )
5. Formidable predators : ( __ , __ )

The treasure is buried at the __ __ __ __ __ in square ( __ , __ ).

⏱ 10

You have **10 minutes** to do this test. Work as quickly and as accurately as you can.

Underline the correct homophone to complete the sentence.

**Example**: Archie tied a _____ in the ship's rigging.     not  <u>knot</u>

1.  Tilly quickly spotted the _____ in the plan.          flaw  floor

2.  Zaynab leant over the _____ of the tour bus.          side  sighed

3.  Marin wrote an action-packed _____ in class.          storey  story

4.  Stuart tried _____ at the seafood restaurant.          muscles  mussels

5.  Callum hung his clothes neatly on a _____.          hanger  hangar

6.  I don't know _____ there will be any pizza.          weather  whether

Mark the word outside the brackets that has a similar meaning to the words in both sets of brackets.

**Example**: (find  discover) (stain  blemish)     freckle  smudge  <u>spot</u>  see

7.  (shaft  ray)          (plank  board)          panel  beam  brace  streak

8.  (amuse  interest)  (host  receive)          invite  charm  distract  entertain

9.  (spark  glint)          (dart  shoot)          flash  blaze  glisten  radiate

10. (reason  motive)  (prompt  trigger)          grounds  produce  cause  originate

11. (hint  clue)          (usher  escort)          lead  trace  signal  dictate

12. (increase  grow)  (climb  ascend)          scale  scramble  mount  stretch

© CGP — not to be photocopied          71          Test 23

Complete the word on the right so that it is an antonym, or nearly an antonym, of the word on the left.

**Example**: smooth   r o u g h

13. assault    d _ f _ _ d

14. outlying    c _ n t _ _ _ l

15. woeful    c _ _ e r _ u _

16. hasten    d _ w _ _ e

17. stingily    g _ n e _ o u _ l _

18. forbidden    a _ _ o w _ d

Underline the word that is the best synonym for the word in bold and makes sense in the sentence.

**Example**: The river was **broad**.    flowing   muddy   <u>wide</u>   fast

19. Brock's drawings of his **fictional** world were fantastic.
    imaginary   magical   enchanted   mysterious

20. Amal **stamped** through the shopping centre behind her parents.
    strode   hiked   clamped   tramped

21. The painting was **clearly** by a talented artist.
    amazingly   obviously   freely   supposedly

22. Miguel's cousin **pestered** his aunt with requests for sweets.
    queried    demanded    harassed    scolded

23. Waiting in queues is extremely **boring**.
    tiresome    eventful    sapping    overtaxing

24. Natalie tripped and fell **awkwardly** on her way to the shops.
    painfully    violently    lightly    inelegantly

25. Swimming is a **relaxing** form of exercise.
    invigorating    soothing    bracing    cosy

**END OF TEST**

/ 25

You have **10 minutes** to do this test. Work as quickly and as accurately as you can.

Find the word that is a synonym, or nearly a synonym, of the word on the left.

**Example**: **wide**    flat    straight    <u>broad</u>    long

1. **miserable**    annoying    irritating    disturbing    wretched

2. **careless**    helpless    watchful    wasteful    reckless

3. **enchant**    appease    delight    elevate    unsettle

4. **disclose**    conceal    reveal    divide    cover

5. **troubling**    mischievous    worrying    incautious    refreshing

6. **create**    distribute    display    devise    advertise

Look at the definition on the left. Underline the word on the right that best matches the definition.

**Example**: to jog slowly      scurry    lunge    sprint    <u>trot</u>

7. to take large steps      stroll    shuffle    stride    saunter

8. a ruler of a country      minister    monarch    lord    dynasty

9. easy to damage      fancy    robust    flowery    flimsy

10. to plot together      conspire    judge    conspiracy    invent

11. to predict      forecast    imagine    see    suspect

12. an angry speech      discussion    bellow    rant    clamour

Complete the word on the right so that it is an antonym, or nearly an antonym, of the word on the left.

**Example**:  smooth          r <u>oug</u> h

13. dispirit          mot_____te

14. expose          disg_____

15. unhealthy          w_____l

16. heedful          u_____ndful

17. save          sq_____er

18. flawless          imp_____ct

19. build          d_____ntle

Choose the correct three-letter word to complete the word in capital letters, so that it finishes the sentence in a sensible way.

**Example**:  It can be **CHY** outside when it snows.

     **APP**       **ILL**       **EEK**       **ERR**
     ☐        ■        ☐        ☐

20. The window **STERED** when the ball hit it.

    **CAT**      **HAT**      **HUT**      **MAT**
    ☐       ☐       ☐       ☐

21. The sun was so bright that I couldn't stop **BLING**.

    **EAT**      **END**      **INK**      **OAT**
    ☐       ☐       ☐       ☐

22. Eshe was **SELESS** about showing off when she won first prize.

**HAD** ☐     **HAM** ☐     **PIN** ☐     **TAT** ☐

23. Ovie **FRS** whenever he has to concentrate hard on something.

**ILL** ☐     **LOO** ☐     **OWN** ☐     **EMU** ☐

24. All the **BERS** on the other team were great at throwing the ball.

**ART** ☐     **OIL** ☐     **OWL** ☐     **RIB** ☐

25. Sarah buys new **CHS** for her bracelet everywhere she travels.

**ARM** ☐     **ORE** ☐     **EAT** ☐     **AIR** ☐

**END OF TEST**

/ 25

                                    © CGP — not to be photocopied

You have **10 minutes** to do this test.  Work as quickly and as accurately as you can.

Mark the word outside the brackets that has a similar meaning to the words in both sets of brackets.

**Example**: (find discover) (stain blemish)    freckle  smudge  <u>spot</u>  see

1.  (begin  establish)    (jolt  jerk)              outset  start  lurch  found

2.  (tube  cylinder)     (wheel  push)           scroll  roll  circle  drum

3.  (dispute  quarrel)   (bang  clang)           clash  clank  clatter  argument

4.  (cherish  adore)     (jewels  riches)         gold  hoard  treasure  wealth

5.  (stump  stub)        (finish  conclusion)     end  puzzle  perplex  close

Complete the word on the right so that it is a synonym, or nearly a synonym, of the word on the left.

**Example**:  rug      <u>car</u>pet

6.  declare          anno_____

7.  fight            c_____bat

8.  abruptly         _____enly

9.  vibrant          b_____t

10. example          mo_____l

Select the most appropriate word from the table to complete each pair of antonyms below. Write the word on the corresponding line.

| innocently | lengthy | courteously | enmity | miniature |
|---|---|---|---|---|
| avoid | chill | indistinct | acknowledge | destruction |

11. clear          _____

12. giant          _____

13. brief          _____

14. creation       _____

15. friendship     _____

16. face           _____

17. rudely         _____

18. guiltily       _____

19. ignore         _____

20. warm           _____

Look at the word on the left. Underline the category that it belongs to.

**Example:**  scarlet          <u>red</u>     yellow     blue     green

21. tent          canvas     circus     shelter     camp

22. tango          action     dance     salsa     instrument

23. bakery          stall     fair     boutique     business

24. nightmare          dream     horror     thought     prank

25. cluster          collection     universe     section     company

**END OF TEST**

/ 25

Break time! These puzzles are great for practising **vocabulary** and **word-making** skills.

## Word Maker

Elvar and Aidan have been fighting over their stash of words. Unfortunately, they've managed to break some of them up. Draw lines to match each white card with the correct ending in the blue cards to create four new words. Some of the cards have more than one possible match, but you can only use each card once. Write the new words on the lines below.

| night | side | _____ |
| in | time | _____ |
| out | box | _____ |
| lunch | cast | _____ |

## Shipshape Words

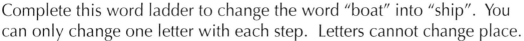

Complete this word ladder to change the word "boat" into "ship". You can only change one letter with each step. Letters cannot change place.

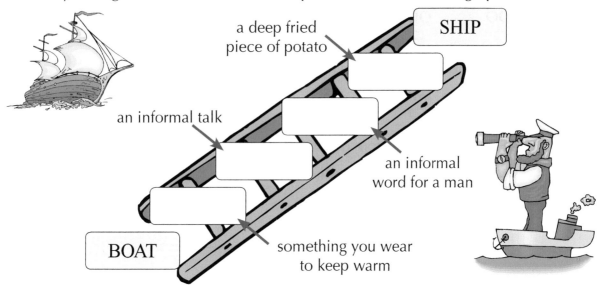

SHIP

a deep fried piece of potato

an informal talk

an informal word for a man

BOAT

something you wear to keep warm

© CGP — not to be photocopied

You have **10 minutes** to do this test.  Work as quickly and as accurately as you can.

Choose the correct three-letter word to complete the word in capital letters, so that it finishes the sentence in a sensible way.

**Example**:  It can be **CHY** outside when it snows.

| APP | ILL | EEK | ERR |
|-----|-----|-----|-----|
| ☐ | ▬ | ☐ | ☐ |

1.  The milk **CON** was completely empty.

| ANY | COO | ART | RAY |
|-----|-----|-----|-----|
| ☐ | ☐ | ☐ | ☐ |

2.  Jonny was much **STER** than his older brother.

| MAR | PAT | HUT | HAT |
|-----|-----|-----|-----|
| ☐ | ☐ | ☐ | ☐ |

3.  The **CERS** were advised to not leave food outside their tents.

| ANT | ALL | AMP | HAS |
|-----|-----|-----|-----|
| ☐ | ☐ | ☐ | ☐ |

4.  Kathy was **SPED** by her grandparents.

| TOO | OUT | NAP | OIL |
|-----|-----|-----|-----|
| ☐ | ☐ | ☐ | ☐ |

5.  Oliver **LED** home after injuring his leg in the marathon.

| AND | IMP | ASH | EGG |
|-----|-----|-----|-----|
| ☐ | ☐ | ☐ | ☐ |

6.  We **TED** the campsite before deciding where to set up our caravan.

| OUR | WIN | AIL | OIL |
|-----|-----|-----|-----|
| ☐ | ☐ | ☐ | ☐ |

© CGP — not to be photocopied

Three of the words in each list are linked. Mark the word
that is not related to these three.

**Example**: teacher   doctor   <u>hospital</u>   firefighter

7.  ornate   fussy   practical   embellished

8.  boar   elephant   walrus   tusk

9.  statue   recording   sculpture   carving

10. armour   shield   knight   sword

11. liquid   sweat   tears   saliva

12. paddling   splashing   swimming   sprinting

Find the word that is an antonym, or nearly an antonym,
of the word on the left.

**Example**: **first**   later   <u>last</u>   next   beginning

13. **unsuitable**   displeasing   unexpected   apt   comfortable

14. **forgive**   enjoy   resent   bolster   dislike

15. **relax**   revise   forget   tighten   neglect

16. **level**   unswerving   stormy   improper   uneven

17. **luck**   misfortune   destiny   trouble   future

18. **similarity**   equality   difference   splitting   separation

Complete the word on the right so that it is a synonym, or nearly a synonym, of the word on the left.

**Example**: rug [c][a][r][p][e][t]

19. await     [e][x][ ][e][c][ ]

20. disease    [p][ ][ ][g][ ][e]

21. repel     [ ][e][p][ ][l][s][ ]

22. change    [a][ ][a][p][ ]

23. witless    [f][ ][o][ ][ ][s][h]

24. knack     [t][a][ ][ ][n][ ]

25. ruin      [d][ ][v][a][ ][t][a][ ][e]

**END OF TEST**

[ / 25 ]

© CGP — not to be photocopied

# Test 27

You have **10 minutes** to do this test.  Work as quickly and as accurately as you can.

Underline the correct homophone to complete the sentence.

    **Example**: Archie tied a _____ in the ship's rigging.    not  <u>knot</u>

1.   May taught the monkey how to _____ a banana.    peel  peal

2.   The small red _____ was spicier than the others.    chilly  chilli

3.   The cross is a _____ of Christianity.    symbol  cymbal

4.   He was the _____ survivor of the shipwreck.    sole  soul

5.   The squirrel climbed up into the _____ tree.    fur  fir

6.   Caden was late to his piano _____.    lesson  lessen

Underline a word from the first set, followed by a word from the second set, that go together to form a new word.

    **Example**: (<u>water</u> suggest disc) (<u>fall</u> hard ton)  (The word is **waterfall**.)

7.   (come  down  fell)    (and  back  low)

8.   (ban  far  air)    (all  in  line)

9.   (set  over  with)    (tea  ride  steed)

10. (sun  row  off)    (shout  deer  roof)

11. (cat  was  wait)    (her  ton  hinge)

12. (under  lost  good)    (less  will  send)

Complete the word on the right so that it is an antonym, or nearly an antonym, of the word on the left.

**Example**: smooth   r o u g h

13. dissatisfied    p ⬚ e a ⬚ ⬚ d

14. joy    ⬚ i s ⬚ r y

15. cowardice    ⬚ o u ⬚ a ⬚ e

16. unguarded    s ⬚ c ⬚ ⬚ e

17. complimentary    c ⬚ i ⬚ i ⬚ a l

18. sicken    r ⬚ c o ⬚ e ⬚

19. omit    i ⬚ c ⬚ ⬚ d e

Underline the word that is the best synonym for the word in bold and makes sense in the sentence.

**Example**: The river was **broad**.    flowing   muddy   <u>wide</u>   fast

20. Catriona felt **uneasy** as she waited outside the head teacher's office.
   terrified    angered    anxious    conflicted

21. The family was **protected** from the storm by a huge boulder.
   renounced    hampered    driven    shielded

22. Martin was praised for his **impeccable** French accent.
   faultless    terrible    convincing    uplifting

23. "Come back here this instant!" **shrieked** the old woman.

    insisted   whispered   prattled   screeched

24. In order to solve this mystery, we must **examine** all the various possibilities.

    exclude   investigate   demonstrate   re-enact

25. Lucy was shocked to see a woman **gazing** at her from an upstairs window.

    mouthing   pouting   grinning   staring


**END OF TEST**

/ 25

Breaktime! This puzzle will help you practise your **word-making** and **vocabulary** skills.

## Precarious Parcel

Bobbi has been asked to grab a parcel from the top shelf but has misjudged the distance. Use the tiles to fill in the gaps below to help Bobbi think of words that mean **balanced** or **secured**. Then, rearrange the remaining tiles to spell out a word that describes how Bobbi is feeling.

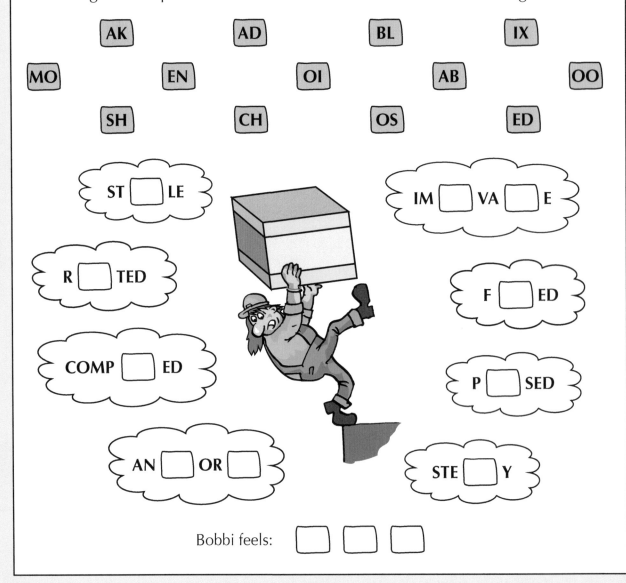

AK   AD   BL   IX

MO   EN   OI   AB   OO

SH   CH   OS   ED

ST ☐ LE

IM ☐ VA ☐ E

R ☐ TED

F ☐ ED

COMP ☐ ED

P ☐ SED

AN ☐ OR ☐

STE ☐ Y

Bobbi feels: ☐ ☐ ☐

86

© CGP — not to be photocopied

(10)

You have **10 minutes** to do this test. Work as quickly and as accurately as you can.

Look at the word on the left. Underline the category that it belongs to.

**Example**: scarlet        <u>red</u>    yellow    blue    green

1. colon      pause    phrase    punctuation    division

2. sight      viewing    sense    smell    vision

3. poppy      blush    flower    redness    sound

4. beach      tide    clifftop    shoreline    pebble

Select the most appropriate word from the table to complete each pair of synonyms below. Write the word on the corresponding line.

| minimise | unafraid | faction | emotional | illogical |
| --- | --- | --- | --- | --- |
| puncture | last | experiment | annoyance | whirl |

5. trial     _____     10. ultimate     _____

6. spin     _____     11. fearless     _____

7. reduce     _____     12. nonsensical     _____

8. sentimental     _____     13. nuisance     _____

9. pierce     _____     14. group     _____

Look at the definition on the left. Underline the word on the right that best matches the definition.

**Example**: to jog slowly          scurry      lunge      sprint      <u>trot</u>

15. a regulation                  guide      suggestion      advice      <u>rule</u>

16. to cut off or obstruct        pursue      <u>intercept</u>      navigate      split

17. made against the law          lethal      <u>outlawed</u>      wrongful      lawless

18. a sudden development          dilemma      <u>breakthrough</u>      chance      moment

19. to shine a light on           <u>illuminate</u>      glaze      purify      enliven

Underline the word that is the best antonym for the word in bold and makes sense in the sentence.

**Example**: Peter found the visit **dull**.          <u>exciting</u>  dreary  upsetting  boring

20. The knight was the most **deserving** soldier in the land.
    respected    <u>unworthy</u>    mediocre    unpopular

21. We had an **inadequate** amount of ingredients to make the soup.
    <u>excessive</u>    incomparable    highlighted    deficient

22. The instructions for assembling the cupboard were in a **random** order.
    confusing    brainless    <u>systematic</u>    unreasonable

23. The engineer couldn't **connect** the train cars.
    strengthen    <u>disengage</u>    disturb    entangle

24. The new novel was praised for its **simplicity**.

method   complexity   clarity   strain

25. Sergio needed help **dismantling** his model aeroplane.

ruining   covering   flying   assembling

**END OF TEST**

/ 25

You have **10 minutes** to do this test. Work as quickly and as accurately as you can.

Three of the words in each list are linked. Mark the word that is not related to these three.

**Example**: teacher   doctor   <u>hospital</u>   firefighter

1. science   history   education   maths

2. clown   acrobat   juggler   engineer

3. anteater   leopard   rabbit   dolphin

4. bland   lazy   idle   inactive

5. ladder   stairs   steps   hatchet

6. limpet   barnacle   seaweed   mussel

Mark the word outside the brackets that has a similar meaning to the words in both sets of brackets.

**Example**: (find discover) (stain blemish)   freckle   smudge   <u>spot</u>   see

7. (chop slice)   (gash wound)   gouge   tear   cut   incision

8. (doubt qualm)   (booking order)   hiring   reservation   worry   concern

9. (bowled threw)   (erected built)   caught   formed   pitched   launched

10. (gutter duct)   (direct transmit)   sending   channel   trough   force

11. (ascent slope)   (bob nod)   jump   incline   leaning   hill

12. (shower bathe)   (clean launder)   wash   laundry   flush   rinse

Complete the word on the right so that it is an antonym,
or nearly an antonym, of the word on the left.

     **Example**: smooth      r <u>oug</u> h

13. interior              ou_____r

14. justice               u_____rness

15. cease                c_____nue

16. fortunate           un_____y

17. mild                  h_____sh

18. unmanageable      con_____able

19. rejection            acce_____ce

Underline the word that is the best synonym for the word in bold and makes
sense in the sentence.

     **Example**: The river was **broad**.     flowing   muddy   <u>wide</u>   fast

20. Kirsty **slackened** the dog's lead so it could run along the beach.
     tightened   pulled   loosened   unhooked

21. The coach was impressed by the footballer's **phenomenal** performance.
     exceptional   lovely   surprising   disappointing

22. She knew it would be **useless** to argue with her friend.
     unusual   crushing   aimless   pointless

23. The mountaineers felt that climbing in this weather would be **unfavourable**.

    unrealistic    disadvantageous    ideal    wise

24. Seydou felt very at home in the **restful** room.

    tranquil    leisurely    jittery    sensitive

25. Petra had difficulty **navigating** the ship past the rocks.

    motoring    manoeuvring    losing    floating

**END OF TEST**

/ 25

Time for a break!  These puzzles are a great way to practise your **vocabulary** skills.

## The Great Swim

Draw a line through the word maze below to help the swimmers find a safe path to the finish line.  The swimmers must only follow paths that spell out words that are **bodies of water**. They can only swim through each square once.

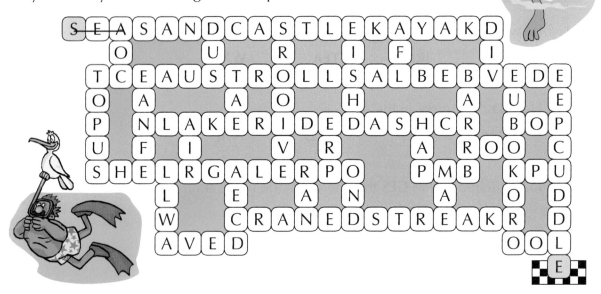

## Across Words

Underline the hidden three-letter word in each sentence.  The hidden word must only cross two words.  The first one has been done for you.

This magical new yo-yo ca**n un**tangle its string without assistance.

The pink flamingo tried to steal our camera.

Victory was clinched thanks to Joe's goal late in the game.

Studying the text helped Maria appreciate the story more.

Chi lifted the sword so high that everyone could see it.

© CGP — not to be photocopied

You have **10 minutes** to do this test.  Work as quickly and as accurately as you can.

Choose the correct three-letter word to complete the word in capital letters, so that it finishes the sentence in a sensible way.

**Example**:  It can be **CHY** outside when it snows.

| APP | ILL | EEK | ERR |
|:---:|:---:|:---:|:---:|
| ☐ | ▬ | ☐ | ☐ |

1.   Bo was **SMING** mischievously at his friend.

| ART | IRK | TEA | WAR |
|:---:|:---:|:---:|:---:|
| ☐ | ☐ | ☐ | ☐ |

2.   He **SED** the cutlery in the drawer.

| HAM | PAR | HAD | TOR |
|:---:|:---:|:---:|:---:|
| ☐ | ☐ | ☐ | ☐ |

3.   Dad stitched up the **GES** that the cat made in the sofa.

| ASH | RIP | RAP | LID |
|:---:|:---:|:---:|:---:|
| ☐ | ☐ | ☐ | ☐ |

4.   The dog **CRED** in the corner.

| ATE | OWE | OWN | AFT |
|:---:|:---:|:---:|:---:|
| ☐ | ☐ | ☐ | ☐ |

5.   Danni **REPED** the tear in her trousers.

| LAY | AIR | ATE | CAP |
|:---:|:---:|:---:|:---:|
| ☐ | ☐ | ☐ | ☐ |

6.   As she got older, the lion cub became **BER**.

| OWL | EAR | LOW | OLD |
|:---:|:---:|:---:|:---:|
| ☐ | ☐ | ☐ | ☐ |

Underline the correct homophone to complete the sentence.

**Example**: Archie tied a _____ in the ship's rigging.    not   <u>knot</u>

7.   Tommy likes to eat _____ for breakfast.    serial   cereal

8.   Bethany led the horse by its _____.    bridal   bridle

9.   The shop _____ birthday cards.    cells   sells

10. Rani _____ advice from his father.    sought   sort

11. The smell of freshly baked _____ filled the room.    bred   bread

12. The man liked to _____ purple shoes.    where   wear

Find the word that is an antonym, or nearly an antonym, of the word on the left.

**Example**: **first**   later   <u>last</u>   next   beginning

13. **rudeness**    nastiness   courtesy   comfort   fairness

14. **distressed**    unconcerned   silent   curious   humble

15. **icy**    parched   scorching   polar   tepid

16. **public**    shared   harmonious   novel   confidential

17. **thrifty**    deafening   extravagant   prudent   buoyant

18. **right**    virtuous   nasty   unethical   heartfelt

Complete the word on the right so that it is a synonym, or nearly a synonym, of the word on the left.

**Example:** rug ___car_pet

19. manufacture      co_____uct

20. positive      upb_____

21. jail      imp_____n

22. brains      inte_____ence

23. wary      ca_____ous

24. study      i_____ect

25. plans      de_____ns

**END OF TEST**

/ 25

© CGP — not to be photocopied

⏱ 10

You have **10 minutes** to do this test.  Work as quickly and as accurately as you can.

Find the word that is a synonym, or nearly a synonym, of the word on the left.

**Example**: **wide**    flat    straight    <u>broad</u>    long

1. **bookish**      formal    volatile    unlearned    studious

2. **nominate**     appoint    eliminate    blame    assist

3. **meagre**       quaint    unsure    insufficient    unlimited

4. **shy**          sharp    kindly    informal    bashful

5. **honesty**      arrogance    toleration    frankness    bravery

6. **control**      disregard    manipulate    accept    garnish

Underline a word from the first set, followed by a word from the second set, that go together to form a new word.

**Example**:  (<u>water</u> suggest disc)  (<u>fall</u> hard ton)    (The word is **waterfall**.)

7.  (photo  crafts  ant)        (cat  den  man)

8.  (some  whole  one)          (when  thing  there)

9.  (fare  more  grass)         (ground  hole  well)

10. (smart  know  dumb)         (most  struck  leap)

11. (arm  bed  hand)            (banned  trench  pit)

12. (purse  pack  bag)          (pipes  clear  hold)

© CGP — not to be photocopied

Mark the word outside the brackets that has a similar meaning to the words in both sets of brackets.

**Example**: (find discover) (stain blemish)     freckle   smudge   <u>spot</u>   see

13. (bog   marsh)        (engulf   swallow)        overrun   flood   mire   swamp

14. (bluffs   fibs)        (reclines   lounges)        sleeps   relaxes   lies   misleads

15. (blob   bead)        (fall   plunge)        tumble   slump   dot   drop

16. (follow   stalk)        (shade   darkness)        black   shadow   murk   trail

17. (load   cargo)        (duty   responsibility)        task   chore   burden   haul

18. (response   reply)   (solution   remedy)        decision   resolve   answer   return

Complete the word on the right so that it is a synonym, or nearly a synonym, of the word on the left.

**Example**: rug   [c][a][r][p][e][t]

19. ingenious        [ ][l][ ][v][e][ ]

20. etch        [e][ ][g][ ][a][v][ ]

21. elation        [ ][a][p][ ][ ][n][ ][s][ ]

22. provide        [ ][u][p][ ][l][y]

23. frailty     ☐ e a ☐ n ☐ s s

24. downplay     ☐ n d ☐ r s t a ☐ e

25. exhausting     t ☐ x i ☐ g

**END OF TEST**

/ 25

© CGP — not to be photocopied

Break time!  These puzzles are a great way to practise your **word-knowledge** skills.

# Wheel of Words

Complete each word below using the letters in the wheel.  Each word must include the letter '**S**'.  You can only use each letter in the wheel once per word.  There might be more than one way you can complete the word.

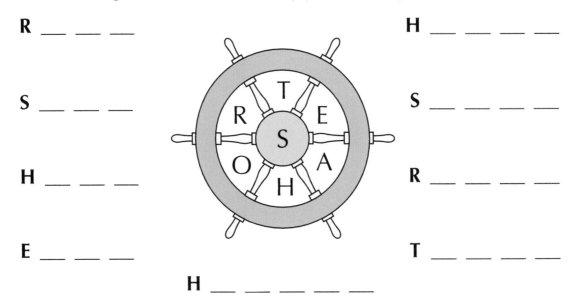

R __ __ __          H __ __ __ __

S __ __ __          S __ __ __ __

H __ __ __          R __ __ __ __

E __ __ __          T __ __ __ __

H __ __ __ __ __

# Problematic Palindromes

There are six words hidden in the grid below that are spelled the same way forwards as they are backwards.  Draw a line through them, then find the one that can be viewed the same forwards, backwards and upside down.

| K | A | Y | A | K | G | F | E | E | T | E | L | E | V | E | L |
| E | M | B | T | O | O | T | D | D | E | E | D | G | Q | A | S |
| H | A | V | E | N | R | J | N | T | U | N | O | O | N | R | I |
| R | E | D | D | E | N | F | I | K | E | L | Y | C | O | O | Z |
| G | O | S | E | L | L | K | W | M | A | D | A | M | M | U | E |

Hint:  This guy's got the right idea.

## Test 1 — pages 2-4

**1. need**
'need' makes sense here — it is the word that means 'require something', whereas 'knead' means 'squeeze with the hands'.

**2. fête**
'fête' makes sense here — it is the word that means 'a collection of stalls', whereas 'fate' means 'destiny'.

**3. steak**
'steak' makes sense here — it is the word that means 'a bit of cooked beef', whereas 'stake' means 'a wooden post'.

**4. leak**
'leak' makes sense here — it is the word that means 'a hole liquid can escape through', whereas a 'leek' is a vegetable.

**5. dough**
'dough' makes sense here — it is the word that describes a mixture used for baking, whereas 'doe' means 'female deer'.

**6. bawled**
'bawled' makes sense here — it is the word that means 'cried', whereas 'bald' means 'having no hair'.

**7. bygone**
Both words mean 'from an earlier time'.

**8. anchorage**
Both words mean 'a place for a ship to anchor'.

**9. worker**
Both words mean 'a person who works for money'.

**10. seep**
Both words mean 'slowly flow out'.

**11. resemblance**
Both words mean 'similarity to someone or something else'.

**12. extension**
Both words mean 'a growth or an enlargement'.

**13. PET**
The complete word is CARPETS.

**14. ANT**
The complete word is CANTER.

**15. ASH**
The complete word is MASHED.

**16. EEL**
The complete word is PEELER.

**17. ORE**
The complete word is SORELY.

**18. ASH**
The complete word is CRASHING.

**19. TOP**
The complete word is STOPPING.

**20. hidden**
'visible' means 'can be seen', whereas 'hidden' means 'not visible'.

**21. overlook**
'notice' means 'to be aware of something', whereas 'overlook' means 'to ignore something'.

**22. imprisoned**
'free' means 'able to go where you like', whereas 'imprisoned' means 'kept captive'.

**23. expected**
'unforeseen' means 'not expected', whereas 'expected' means 'likely to happen'.

**24. proven**
'untested' means 'not shown to be true', whereas 'proven' means 'shown to be true'.

**25. unfasten**
'clamp' means 'tightly fasten', whereas 'unfasten' means 'undo'.

## Test 2 — pages 5-6

**1. whisker**
The other three are parts of animal feet.

**2. accessory**
The other three are pieces of jewellery.

**3. beetroot**
The other three are orange foods.

**4. pelican**
The other three are mammals.

**5. helipad**
The other three are things that fly.

**6. amplified**
'lessened' means 'made less', whereas 'amplified' means 'increased'.

**7. ensnare**
'release' mean 'set free', whereas 'ensnare' means 'capture'.

**8. ascension**
'descent' means 'going down', whereas 'ascension' means 'going up'.

**9. extensive**
'small' means 'not large', whereas 'extensive' means 'large'.

**10. compulsory**
'voluntary' means 'done by choice', whereas 'compulsory' means 'done because you have to'.

**11. surpassed**
'outdid' and 'surpassed' both mean 'did better than expected'.

**12. bitter**
'resentful' and 'bitter' both mean 'showing or feeling anger'.

**13. enduring**

'long-lasting' and 'enduring' both mean 'going on for a long time'.

**14. refusal**

'denial' and 'refusal' both mean 'rejection'.

**15. tuneful**

'melodic' and 'tuneful' both mean 'pleasant to listen to'.

**16. veiled**

'concealed' and 'veiled' both mean 'hidden'.

**17. indignantly**

'angrily' and 'indignantly' both mean 'in an angry way'.

**18. alleviate**

'soothe' and 'alleviate' both mean 'make better'.

**19. appreciate**

'understand' and 'appreciate' both mean 'grasp the meaning of something'.

**20. obstruction**

'blockage' and 'obstruction' both mean 'something that gets in the way'.

**21. glaring**

'glaring' can mean 'clear' or 'staring hard'.

**22. correct**

'correct' can mean 'accurate' or 'put something right'.

**23. trunk**

'trunk' can mean 'the top part of someone's body' or 'a box used to store things'.

**24. cover**

'shelter' can mean 'to shelter from harm' or 'packaging that protects an item'.

**25. step**

'step' can mean 'a stair' or 'a stage in a process'.

## Puzzles 1 — page 7

### Fishing for Words

3-letter words: e.g. **ill**, **how**, **owl**, **hop**, **row**, **rip**, **lip**, **low**
4-letter words: e.g. **hill**, **pool**, **wool**, **pill**, **hoop**, **whip**, **howl**, **will**
5-letter words: e.g. **prowl**, **whirl**
6-letter words: e.g. **hollow**, **pillow**
The 9-letter word is **whirlpool**

## Test 3 — pages 8-10

**1. install**

'install' is the only correctly spelled word that can be made.

**2. sunlight**

'sunlight' is the only correctly spelled word that can be made.

**3. headline**

'headline' is the only correctly spelled word that can be made.

**4. buttercup**

'buttercup' is the only correctly spelled word that can be made.

**5. sideways**

'sideways' is the only correctly spelled word that can be made.

**6. breakdown**

'breakdown' is the only correctly spelled word that can be made.

**7. drumstick**

'drumstick' is the only correctly spelled word that can be made.

**8. helpful**

'uncooperative' means 'unwilling to help', whereas 'helpful' means 'giving help'.

**9. unbuckle**

'fasten' means 'to do up', whereas 'unbuckle' means 'to undo'.

**10. outgoing**

'incoming' means 'coming in', whereas 'outgoing' means 'going out'.

**11. unremarkable**

'extraordinary' means 'unusual', whereas 'unremarkable' means 'ordinary'.

**12. keep**

'relinquish' means 'give up', whereas 'keep' can mean 'hold on to'.

**13. disadvantages**

'merits' means 'advantages', whereas 'disadvantages' means 'downsides'.

**14. thrive**

Both words mean 'to flourish and grow well'.

**15. disorder**

Both words mean 'confusion'.

**16. secretly**

Both words mean 'in secret'.

**17. connected**

Both words mean 'linked'.

**18. dishearten**

Both words mean 'to make someone lose confidence'.

**19. despise**

Both words mean 'to strongly dislike'.

**20. house**

A 'mansion' is a 'house' — it's a large or grand home.

**21. metal**

'copper' is a 'metal' — it's used in coins.

**22. emotion**

'fury' is an 'emotion' — it means 'anger'.

© CGP — not to be photocopied

**23. spread**

'butter' is a 'spread' — it's something you can spread on food.

**24. performer**

A 'magician' is a 'performer' — they perform magic tricks.

**25. stone**

'marble' is a 'stone' — it is often used in buildings or artwork.

# Test 4 — pages 11-13

**1. juice**

The other three are dairy products.

**2. disloyal**

The other three mean 'reliable'.

**3. carpet**

The other three go on a bed.

**4. ruler**

The other three mean 'to fasten with glue'.

**5. conquest**

The other three mean 'award'.

**6. fort**

The other three are places where you can be locked up.

**7. flew**

'flew' makes sense here — it means 'travelled by air', whereas 'flu' means 'a cold-like illness'.

**8. waste**

'waste' makes sense here — it means 'to use carelessly', whereas 'waist' is part of the body.

**9. roar**

'roar' makes sense here — it is a noise an animal makes, whereas 'raw' means 'uncooked'.

**10. savour**

'savour' makes sense here — it means 'enjoy the taste', whereas 'saver' means 'someone who saves money'.

**11. idle**

'idle' makes sense here — it means 'inactive', whereas 'idol' means 'something that is worshipped or admired'.

**12. loan**

'loan' makes sense here — it means 'money that is borrowed', whereas 'lone' means 'on its own'.

**13. shoo**

'shoo' makes sense here — it means 'to usher away', whereas 'shoe' is something you wear on your feet.

**14. assertive**

Both words mean 'confident'.

**15. abuses**

Both words mean 'misuses'.

**16. garments**

Both words mean 'items of clothing'.

**17. enthralling**

Both words mean 'fascinating'.

**18. considerable**

Both words mean 'large'.

**19. bunch**

Both words mean 'a collection'.

**20. embrace**

'embrace' means 'to hug closely'.

**21. reap**

'reap' means 'to harvest a crop'.

**22. aid**

'aid' means 'help or assistance'.

**23. terminate**

'terminate' means 'to put a stop to'.

**24. plummet**

'plummet' means 'to fall quickly'.

**25. elongate**

'elongate' means 'to lengthen'.

# Puzzles 2 — page 14

**Treasure Trail Teaser**

*Location of the treasure:* under the stairs.

# Test 5 — pages 15-17

**1. forget**
'forget' is the only correctly spelled word that can be made.

**2. standby**
'standby' is the only correctly spelled word that can be made.

**3. carpet**
'carpet' is the only correctly spelled word that can be made.

**4. manage**
'manage' is the only correctly spelled word that can be made.

**5. showcase**
'showcase' is the only correctly spelled word that can be made.

**6. tasteless**
'tasteless' is the only correctly spelled word that can be made.

**7. boat**
A 'kayak' is a 'boat' — it is a type of canoe.

**8. language**
'Welsh' is a 'language' — it is mainly spoken in Wales.

**9. teacher**
A 'tutor' is a 'teacher' — tutors often teach students individually.

**10. level**
A 'basement' is a 'level' — it is the floor of a building that is located underneath the ground floor.

**11. accommodation**
A 'hotel' is a kind of 'accommodation' — 'accommodation' means 'place to stay'.

**12. meat**
'pork' is a 'meat' — it comes from pigs.

**13. peaceful**
'violent' means 'aggressive', whereas 'peaceful' means 'not violent'.

**14. finish**
'commence' means 'begin', whereas 'finish' means 'end'.

**15. unearth**
'bury' means 'cover in earth', whereas 'unearth' means 'dig up'.

**16. dull**
'fascinating' means 'interesting', whereas 'dull' means 'boring'.

**17. effective**
'unsuccessful' means 'not succeeding', whereas 'effective' means 'working well'.

**18. approachable**
'unfriendly' means 'not friendly', whereas 'approachable' means 'friendly'.

**19. enlarge**
'shrink' means 'make smaller', whereas 'enlarge' means 'make bigger'.

**20. unexceptional**
'unexceptional' makes sense here — 'ordinary' and 'unexceptional' both mean 'normal'.

**21. significant**
'significant' makes sense here — 'substantial' and 'significant' both mean 'large'.

**22. lasting**
'lasting' makes sense here — 'permanent' and 'lasting' both mean 'long-lasting'.

**23. displaying**
'displaying' makes sense here — 'exhibiting' and 'displaying' both mean 'showing'.

**24. onlookers**
'onlookers' makes sense here — 'bystanders' and 'onlookers' both mean 'people who are watching something'.

**25. solve**
'solve' makes sense here — 'decipher' and 'solve' both mean 'figure out'.

# Test 6 — pages 18-19

**1. timetable**
'timetable' is the only correctly spelled word that can be made.

**2. highway**
'highway' is the only correctly spelled word that can be made.

**3. warlock**
'warlock' is the only correctly spelled word that can be made.

**4. triplet**
'triplet' is the only correctly spelled word that can be made.

**5. humour**
'humour' is the only correctly spelled word that can be made.

**6. submerged**
'submerged' means 'covered by water'.

**7. abundance**
'abundance' means 'a large amount'.

**8. nocturnal**
'nocturnal' means 'active at night'.

**9. graze**
'graze' means 'to scrape the skin'.

**10. feeble**
'feeble' means 'lacking strength'.

**11. undermine**
'support' means 'make stronger', whereas 'undermine' means 'make weaker'.

**12. qualified**
'unskilled' means 'not skilled', whereas 'qualified' means 'skilled'.

**13. adaptable**
'inflexible' means 'unwilling to change', whereas 'adaptable' means 'willing to change'.

**14. wither**
'flourish' means 'to grow strong', whereas 'wither' means 'to become weak'.

**15. disagreeable**
'pleasant' means 'nice', whereas 'disagreeable' means 'not nice'.

**16. turmoil**
'tranquillity' means 'calm', whereas 'turmoil' means 'chaos'.

© CGP — not to be photocopied

**17. original**
'fake' means 'a copy', whereas 'original' means 'the first one'.

**18. dismayed**
'delighted' means 'made happy by something', whereas 'dismayed' means 'made sad by something'.

**19. final**
'introductory' means 'at the beginning', whereas 'final' means 'at the end'.

**20. necessary**
'needless' means 'not needed', whereas 'necessary' means 'needed'.

**21. initiate**
Both words mean 'start'.

**22. hesitate**
Both words mean 'wait for a moment'.

**23. monitor**
Both words mean 'keep track of something'.

**24. expedition**
Both words mean 'a journey'.

**25. trudge**
Both words mean 'walk slowly and heavily'.

# Test 7 — pages 20-22

**1. grasping**
Both words mean 'really wanting something you don't need'.

**2. nurse**
Both words mean 'to care for'.

**3. competence**
Both words mean 'ability to do something'.

**4. motionless**
Both words mean 'not moving'.

**5. routinely**
Both words mean 'frequently'.

**6. win**
Both words mean 'a successful result'.

**7. driveway**
The other three are parts of a car.

**8. risky**
The other three mean 'scary'.

**9. suspend**
The other three mean 'to move forward'.

**10. orchestra**
The other three are musical instruments.

**11. reporter**
The other three are people involved in football matches.

**12. shell**
The other three are types of small stones .

**13. unclear**
'coherent' means 'clear and well reasoned', whereas 'unclear' means 'not easy to understand'.

**14. carelessly**
'thoroughly' means 'with great care', whereas 'carelessly' means 'without care'.

**15. important**
'insignificant' means 'not of great value', whereas 'important' means 'of great value'.

**16. genuine**
'forged' means 'fake', whereas 'genuine' means 'authentic'.

**17. downplayed**
'exaggerated' means 'made something seem worse than it is', whereas 'downplayed' means 'made something seem less important than it is'.

**18. incorrect**
'accurate' means 'correct', whereas 'incorrect' means 'wrong'.

**19. shine**
'shine' can mean 'give off light' or 'to buff up'.

**20. remains**
'remains' can mean 'leftover parts' or 'stays in the same place'.

**21. snatch**
'snatch' can mean 'to take something quickly' or 'a small part of something'.

**22. career**
'career' can mean 'the job someone does' or 'to move in a quick and uncontrolled way'.

**23. float**
'float' can mean 'an object that doesn't sink' or 'to move slowly in the air or in a liquid'.

**24. empty**
'empty' can mean 'to remove all contents' or 'to contain nothing'.

**25. pass**
'pass' can mean 'to come to an end' or 'to give something to another person'.

# Puzzles 3 — page 23

## Odds and Ends

**The odd words are:** blue, ear, bell, foot, wash, wall, drum, bridge, paper, bed, brain, room
**Compound words:** bluebell, eardrum, footbridge, wallpaper, bedroom, brainwash

# Test 8 — pages 24-26

**1. ARM**
The complete word is HARMED.

**2. SEE**
The complete word is UNSEEN.

**3. RIB**
The complete word is BRIBING.

**4. RUT**
The complete word is TRUTHS.

**5. CUT**
The complete word is SCUTTLE.

**6. OIL**
The complete word is BOILER.

**7. livestock**
A 'sheep' is a type of 'livestock' — 'livestock' are farm animals.

**8. ruler**
A 'queen' is a 'ruler' — it is a woman who rules a country.

**9. tool**
A 'chisel' is a 'tool' — it is used to cut hard materials.

**10. shoes**
'trainers' are 'shoes' — they are worn on the feet.

**11. tree**
'willow' is a type of 'tree'.

**12. organ**
A 'heart' is an 'organ' — an 'organ' is something inside the body which performs a function.

**13. luggage**
A 'suitcase' is a type of 'luggage' — 'luggage' is something used to pack belongings in for travelling.

**14. accidental**
'intentional' means 'on purpose', whereas 'accidental' means 'by accident'.

**15. excess**
'moderation' means 'in reasonable amounts', whereas 'excess' means 'more than what is needed'.

**16. vertical**
'horizontal' means 'going across', whereas vertical means 'going up and down'.

**17. flatter**
'insult' means 'to be mean to', whereas 'flatter' means 'to compliment'.

**18. dwindle**
'increase' means 'to get bigger', whereas 'dwindle' means 'to get smaller'.

**19. rebel**
'conform' means 'to follow the accepted rules', whereas 'rebel' can mean 'to go against the rules'.

**20. eatable**
Both words mean 'okay to eat'.

**21. adamant**
Both words mean 'determined'.

**22. fitting**
Both words mean 'right for something'.

**23. exchange**
Both words mean 'to swap'.

**24. improve**
Both words mean 'to make better'.

**25. maintenance**
Both words mean 'work done to keep something in good condition'.

# Test 9 — pages 27-29

**1. shear**
'shear' makes sense here — it is the word that means 'to cut off wool', whereas 'sheer' means 'very thin'.

**2. whine**
'whine' makes sense here — it is the word that means 'make a high-pitched sound', whereas 'wine' means 'an alcoholic drink'.

**3. urn**
'urn' makes sense here — it is the word that means 'a vase', whereas 'earn' means 'to gain through effort'.

**4. council**
'council' makes sense here — it is the word that means 'an elected group of people', whereas 'counsel' means 'to give advice'.

**5. loot**
'loot' makes sense here — it is the word that means 'steal', whereas 'lute' means 'a stringed instrument'.

**6. creek**
'creek' makes sense here — it is the word that means 'a small stream', whereas 'creak' means 'a squeaking sound'.

**7. ignite**
'ignite' means 'to set on fire'.

**8. excavate**
'excavate' means 'to dig out'.

**9. peculiarity**
'peculiarity' means 'a strange thing'.

**10. conceited**
'conceited' means 'self-obsessed'.

**11. twitch**
'twitch' means 'to jerk suddenly'.

**12. elect**
'elect' means 'to vote someone in'.

**13. grimace**
Both words can mean 'to frown'.

**14. faithful**
Both words can mean 'true to the facts'.

**15. heartless**
Both words can mean 'unfeeling'.

© CGP — not to be photocopied

**16. courageous**

Both words can mean 'brave'.

**17. vibrate**

Both words can mean 'to move quickly to and fro'.

**18. withstand**

Both words can mean 'to oppose'.

**19. permit**

Both words can mean 'a document that shows you are allowed to do something'.

**20. occupied**

'vacant' means 'empty', whereas 'occupied' means 'in use'.

**21. certain**

'undecided' means 'not sure', whereas 'certain' means 'sure'.

**22. offensive**

'defensive' means 'readiness to defend', whereas 'offensive' can mean 'readiness to act aggressively'.

**23. exciting**

'tedious' means 'boring', whereas 'exciting' means 'thrilling'.

**24. confined**

'spacious' means 'having a lot of space', whereas 'confined' means 'not having much space'.

**25. established**

'new' means 'recently developed', whereas 'established' means 'having existed for a long time'.

# Test 10 — pages 30-31

**1. approach**

'approach' can mean 'a way of handling a situation' or 'an access road leading to a place'.

**2. chance**

'chance' can mean 'how likely it is that something will happen' or 'an opportunity'.

**3. craft**

'craft' can mean 'the ability to make things by hand' or 'a water vessel'.

**4. remote**

'remote' can mean 'a long way away' or 'not likely'.

**5. twist**

'twist' can mean 'to rotate' or 'to bend out of shape'.

**6. notebook**

'notebook' is the only correctly spelled word that can be made.

**7. daredevil**

'daredevil' is the only correctly spelled word that can be made.

**8. grasshopper**

'grasshopper' is the only correctly spelled word that can be made.

**9. landslide**

'landslide' is the only correctly spelled word that can be made.

**10. footwear**

'footwear' is the only correctly spelled word that can be made.

**11. utterly**

'completely' and 'utterly' both mean 'totally'.

**12. feasible**

'possible' and 'feasible' both mean 'able to be done'.

**13. grieve**

'mourn' and 'grieve' both mean 'to feel very sad about a loss'.

**14. order**

'tidiness' and 'order' both mean 'neatness'.

**15. vigilant**

'alert' and 'vigilant' both mean 'watching for potential danger'.

**16. booming**

'successful' and 'booming' both mean 'doing well'.

**17. possibly**

'potentially' and 'possibly' both mean 'with the ability to happen'.

**18. modernise**

'update' and 'modernise' both mean 'to bring up to date'.

**19. confusion**

'disarray' and 'confusion' both mean 'a state of disorder'.

**20. implore**

'beg' and 'implore' both mean 'to plead'.

**21. disappoint**

'satisfy' means 'to meet expectations', whereas 'disappoint' means 'to not fulfil expectations'.

**22. weaken**

'fortify' means 'strengthen', whereas 'weaken' means 'to make weaker'.

**23. thoughtful**

'tactless' means 'not thinking about the feelings of others', whereas 'thoughtful' means 'thinking of others'.

**24. divided**

'united' means 'joined together', whereas 'divided' means 'in disagreement'.

**25. background**

'foreground' means 'the area at the front of an image', whereas 'background' means 'the area in the back of an image'.

# Puzzles 4 — page 32

**The Pirate's Code**

**The treasure is located:** UNDER THE COCONUT TREE WITH EIGHT LEAVES

**Lose a Letter**

beak, brow, fiend

# Test 11 — pages 33-35

## 1. plain
'plain' makes sense here — it is the word that means 'an area of flat land', whereas 'plane' means 'an aircraft'.

## 2. quay
'quay' makes sense here — it is the word that means 'a platform next to water', whereas 'key' is the word that describes a device for unlocking doors.

## 3. build
'build' makes sense here — it means 'construct', whereas 'billed' means 'having a beak'.

## 4. weight
'weight' makes sense here — it means 'the heaviness of something', whereas 'wait' means 'to hold back from doing something'.

## 5. current
'current' makes sense here — it is the word that means 'the movement of water', whereas a 'currant' is a dried fruit.

## 6. place
'place' makes sense here — it is the word that means 'location', whereas 'plaice' is a type of fish.

## 7. slip
'slip' can mean 'a minor error' or 'to move without attracting attention'.

## 8. caring
'caring' can mean 'loving' or 'looking after'.

## 9. pinch
'pinch' can mean 'grab something tightly' or 'a small amount'.

## 10. cycle
'cycle' can mean 'a repeated chain of events' or 'an action used to ride a bike'.

## 11. bargain
'bargain' can mean 'an agreement between two groups or people' or 'to negotiate'.

## 12. grow
'grow' can mean 'develop' or 'become larger'.

## 13. frequently
'rarely' means 'not happening very often', whereas 'frequently' means 'happening a lot'.

## 14. validate
'disprove' means 'show something is false', whereas 'validate' means 'prove something is true'.

## 15. neglectful
'careful' means 'with care and attention', whereas 'neglectful' means 'without care and attention'.

## 16. incapable
'able' means 'can do something', whereas 'incapable' means 'unable to do something'.

## 17. frostiness
'warmth' means 'heat', whereas 'frostiness' means 'coldness'.

## 18. forgettable
'memorable' means 'easy to remember', whereas 'forgettable' means 'easy to forget'.

## 19. strict
'easygoing' means 'relaxed about things', whereas 'strict' means 'demanding that rules are followed'.

## 20. puzzling
'puzzling' makes sense here — 'bewildering' and 'puzzling' both mean 'confusing'.

## 21. tempting
'tempting' makes sense here — 'appetising' and 'tempting' both mean 'appealing'.

## 22. relieve
'relieve' makes sense here — 'cure' and 'relieve' both mean 'make better'.

## 23. punishing
'punishing' makes sense here — 'strenuous' and 'punishing' both mean 'difficult'.

## 24. zest
'zest' makes sense here — 'keenness' and 'zest' both mean 'a desire for something'.

## 25. unblemished
'unblemished' makes sense here — 'unblemished' and 'untarnished' both mean 'without marks'.

# Test 12 — pages 36-38

## 1. RAP
The complete word is DRAPING.

## 2. ASH
The complete word is WASHING.

## 3. ADD
The complete word is LADDER.

## 4. ARE
The complete word is CAREER.

## 5. ROW
The complete word is PROWLS.

## 6. carefully
'clumsily' means 'without care', whereas 'carefully' means 'with care'.

## 7. fresh
'musty' means 'stale', whereas 'fresh' means 'new'.

## 8. rough
'sleek' means 'smooth', whereas 'rough' means 'not smooth'.

## 9. favourite
'underdog' means 'a person not likely to win', whereas 'favourite' can mean 'a person likely to win'.

## 10. slightly
'extremely' means 'to a large degree', whereas 'slightly' means 'to a small degree'.

© CGP — not to be photocopied

**11. collected**

'panicky' means 'uncontrollably afraid', whereas 'collected' means 'calm and in control'.

**12. heighten**

'dampen' means 'make less intense', whereas 'heighten' means 'get more intense'.

**13. moisten**

'dry' means 'remove moisture from', whereas 'moisten' means 'make wet'.

**14. disagree**

'consent' means 'agree to something', whereas 'disagree' means 'not agree with something'.

**15. reduction**

'enlargement' means 'a growth', whereas 'reduction' means 'a lessening'.

**16. jealous**

Both words mean 'resenting others for what they have'.

**17. flicker**

Both words mean 'a faint light'.

**18. manual**

Both words mean 'a book of instructions'.

**19. unknowing**

Both words mean 'not aware of something'.

**20. parade**

Both words mean 'a procession'.

**21. painting**

A 'watercolour' is a 'painting' — it is created using watercolour paint.

**22. distance**

A 'mile' is a 'distance' — it is used to measure how far something has travelled.

**23. cereal**

'Wheat' is a type of 'cereal' — a cereal is a grain that can be made into food.

**24. dessert**

A 'strudel' is a 'dessert' — it is a pastry that contains fruit.

**25. aircraft**

A 'helicopter' is an 'aircraft' — it uses rotor blades to help it fly through the air.

# Test 13 — pages 39-41

**1. dislike**

'fondness' means 'a liking for something', whereas 'dislike' means 'a lack of liking for something'.

**2. reliable**

'undependable' means 'not able to be relied on', whereas 'reliable' means 'able to be relied on'.

**3. belated**

'early' means 'before the expected time', whereas 'belated' means 'after the expected time'.

**4. forgiving**

'merciless' means 'without mercy', whereas 'forgiving' means 'willing to show mercy'.

**5. decide**

'dither' means 'fail to make a decision', whereas 'decide' means 'make a decision'.

**6. disciplined**

'uncontrolled' means 'without control', whereas 'disciplined' can mean 'with control'.

**7. distracted**

'focussed' means 'paying attention to what you're doing', whereas 'distracted' means 'not paying attention'.

**8. bolt**

The other three mean 'to walk slowly'.

**9. fine**

The other three refer to bad weather.

**10. reindeer**

The other three are birds.

**11. settler**

The other three refer to people who travel around.

**12. soft**

The other three are types of fabric.

**13. complete**

The other three mean 'to think about'.

**14. illegible**

'illegible' makes sense here — 'unreadable' and 'illegible' both mean 'impossible to read'.

**15. playing**

'playing' makes sense here — 'frolicking' and 'playing both mean 'playing happily'.

**16. meddling**

'meddling' makes sense here — 'tampering' and 'meddling' both mean 'interfering'.

**17. ignorant**

'ignorant' makes sense here — 'unaware' and 'ignorant' both mean 'not knowing about something'.

**18. yearning**

'yearning' makes sense here — 'longing' and 'yearning' both mean 'really wanting'.

**19. viable**

'viable' makes sense here — 'workable' and 'viable' both mean 'possible'.

**20. inept**

'inept' means 'having no skill'.

**21. endure**

'endure' means 'to put up with'.

**22. reiterate**

'reiterate' means 'to say again'.

**23. feud**

'feud' means 'an ongoing fight'.

**24. pristine**

'pristine' means 'as good as new'.

**25. boisterous**

'boisterous' means 'lively and noisy'.

# Puzzles 5 — page 42

## The Great Escape

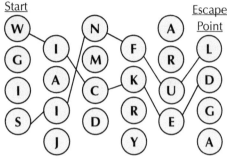

Start           Escape Point

## Riddle Me This

**Answer to the riddle:** Time

# Test 14 — pages 43-45

**1. END**

The complete word is TENDING.

**2. ACT**

The complete word is REACTED.

**3. OWL**

The complete word is SLOWLY.

**4. OAT**

The complete word is FLOATED.

**5. KIN**

The complete word is UNKIND.

**6. LAY**

The complete word is DELAYED.

**7. disorganised**

'orderly' means 'well organised', whereas 'disorganised' means 'not organised'.

**8. calm**

'restless' means 'not relaxed', whereas 'calm' means 'relaxed'.

**9. confident**

'doubtful' means 'uncertain about something', whereas 'confident' means 'feeling certain'.

**10. cowardly**

'bold' means 'brave', whereas 'cowardly' means 'lacking courage'.

**11. peculiar**

'normal' means 'ordinary', whereas 'peculiar' means 'out of the ordinary'.

**12. hindrance**

'assistance' means 'help', whereas 'hindrance' means 'something that gets in the way'.

**13. rotten**

'rotten' is the only correctly spelled word that can be made.

**14. bargain**

'bargain' is the only correctly spelled word that can be made.

**15. earwax**

'earwax' is the only correctly spelled word that can be made.

**16. offend**

'offend' is the only correctly spelled word that can be made.

**17. ordeal**

'ordeal' is the only correctly spelled word that can be made.

**18. flagpole**

'flagpole' is the only correctly spelled word that can be made.

**19. dreary**

Both words mean 'dull and miserable'.

**20. suppose**

Both words mean 'take something to be true without proof'.

**21. amazing**

Both words mean 'remarkable'.

**22. sensible**
Both words mean 'acting in a way that's reasonable'.

**23. repeat**
Both words mean 'do something again'.

**24. locate**
Both words mean 'to work out where something is'.

**25. match**
Both words mean 'a thing that is the same as another thing'.

# Test 15 — pages 46-48

**1. enable**
Both words mean 'let something happen'.

**2. trickle**
Both words mean 'drip'.

**3. injure**
Both words mean 'hurt'.

**4. determination**
Both words mean 'a strong will'.

**5. worthwhile**
Both words mean 'worth doing'.

**6. persistent**
Both words mean 'never-ending'.

**7. goal**
The other three are outcomes of a sports match.

**8. moss**
The other three are green foods.

**9. designer**
The other three are types of pictures.

**10. grouping**
The other three are used to describe social gatherings.

**11. kidnap**
The other three mean 'take without permission'.

**12. supplier**
The other three are people who buy goods.

**13. defence**
A 'drawbridge' is a 'defence' — it stops attackers from getting into a castle.

**14. substance**
'wax' is a 'substance' — it is used in candles.

**15. continent**
'Europe' is a 'continent' — it is a large group of countries.

**16. fee**
A 'toll' is a 'fee' — it is something you have to pay.

**17. season**
'winter' is a 'season' — it is a period of the year.

**18. trick**
A 'prank' is a 'trick' — it's a joke you play on someone else.

**19. scarce**
Both words mean 'not common'.

**20. enthusiasm**
Both words mean 'a will to do something'.

**21. habitat**
Both words mean 'a place where something lives'.

**22. superior**
Both words mean 'more excellent'.

**23. steer**
Both words mean 'guide a vehicle'.

**24. voyage**
Both words mean 'trip'.

**25. daring**
Both words mean 'willing to take risks'.

# Test 16 — pages 49-51

**1. islet**
'islet' means 'a little island'.

**2. participate**
'participate' means 'to join in'.

**3. idolise**
'idolise' means 'to admire a lot'.

**4. spineless**
'spineless' means 'weak and cowardly'.

**5. banquet**
'banquet' means 'an extravagant meal'.

**6. discover**
'discover' means 'to find out'.

**7. playlist**
'playlist' is the only correctly spelled word that can be made.

**8. drawback**
'drawback' is the only correctly spelled word that can be made.

**9. handmade**
'handmade' is the only correctly spelled word that can be made.

**10. bearable**
'bearable' is the only correctly spelled word that can be made.

**11. foresee**
'foresee' is the only correctly spelled word that can be made.

**12. upon**
'upon' is the only correctly spelled word that can be made.

**13. rest**
'toil' means 'hard work', whereas 'rest' means 'relaxing'.

**14. closed**
'ajar' means 'slightly open', whereas 'closed' means 'shut'.

**15. shameless**
'ashamed' means 'feeling embarrassed or guilty', whereas 'shameless' means 'having no sense of shame'.

**16. stability**

'insecurity' can mean 'not stable', whereas 'stability' means 'being stable'.

**17. steadily**

'shakily' means 'while shaking', whereas 'steadily' can mean 'without shaking'.

**18. simplify**

'complicate' means 'make more complex', whereas 'simplify' means 'make more straightforward'.

**19. succeed**

'fail' means 'not achieve an aim', whereas 'succeed' means 'achieve an aim'.

**20. invigorated**

'exhausted' means 'very tired', whereas 'invigorated' means 'given energy'.

**21. displeasure**

'satisfaction' means 'happiness with something', whereas 'displeasure' means 'disappointment with something'.

**22. bored**

'fascinated' means 'very interested', whereas 'bored' can mean 'not at all interested'.

**23. casually**

'formally' can mean 'properly and in line with the rules', whereas 'casually' means 'in a relaxed way'.

**24. rigorous**

'gentle' can mean 'not requiring much effort', whereas 'rigorous' can mean 'requiring lots of effort'.

**25. rapidly**

'slowly' means 'not quickly', whereas 'rapidly' means 'quickly'.

## Puzzles 6 — page 52

### Homophone Hunt

dressing for food — **sauce** (source); place after third — **fourth** (forth); a solemn pledge — **pact** (packed); interfere — **meddle** (medal); a smell — **scent** (sent); there are seven in a week — **days** (daze)

## Test 17 — pages 53-54

**1. aloud**

'aloud' makes sense here — it is the word that means 'out loud', whereas 'allowed' means 'permitted'.

**2. mousse**

'mousse' makes sense here — it is a type of pudding, whereas 'moose' is a large type of deer.

**3. reek**

'reek' makes sense here — it is the word that means 'smell bad', whereas 'wreak' means 'cause harm'.

**4. vain**

'vain' makes sense here — it is the word that means 'having too much pride in yourself', whereas 'vein' is a type of blood vessel.

**5. pried**

'pried' makes sense here — it is the word that means 'to get something with difficulty', whereas 'pride' means 'feeling good about yourself'.

**6. beyond**

'beyond' can mean 'extending further than' or 'greater than'.

**7. champion**

'champion' can mean 'to defend and stand up for' or 'winner'.

**8. escape**

'escape' can mean 'to run away' or 'to avoid doing'.

**9. short**

'short' can mean 'little in height or length' or 'lasting a small amount of time'.

**10. squat**

'squat' can mean 'to lower yourself to the ground by bending your knees' or 'short and wide'.

**11. tame**

'ferocious' can mean 'fierce and violent', whereas 'tame' means 'not dangerous'.

**12. lose**

'acquire' means 'to get something', whereas 'lose' means 'to stop having something'.

**13. conquered**

'liberated' means 'freed', whereas 'conquered' means 'taken over by force'.

**14. demote**

'promote' means 'raise to a higher rank', whereas 'demote' means 'move to a lower rank'.

**15. hatred**

'love' means 'a strong feeling of affection', whereas 'hatred' means 'an extreme feeling of dislike'.

**16. thoughtless**

'considerate' means 'mindful', whereas 'thoughtless' means 'without thinking'.

**17. modern**

'outdated' means 'old-fashioned', whereas 'modern' means 'up to date'.

**18. demotivated**

'energised' means 'made to feel enthusiastic about something', whereas 'demotivated' means 'made to feel less eager to do something'.

**19. truth**

'fiction' can mean 'something that is untrue', whereas 'truth' means 'something that is factually correct'.

**20. lengthen**

'condense' can mean 'to make something shorter', whereas 'lengthen' means 'to make something longer'.

**21. benefit**

Both words can mean 'a good feature or point'.

**22. volunteer**

Both words can mean 'to offer freely or willingly'.

**23. chilling**

Both words can mean 'frightening'.

**24. margin**

Both words can mean 'edge'.

**25. defensive**

Both words can mean 'having a desire to keep someone or something safe'.

# Test 18 — pages 55-57

**1. RAT**

The complete word is GRATER.

**2. EAR**

The complete word is WEARING.

**3. FAN**

The complete word is INFANT.

**4. MEN**

The complete word is AMENDS.

**5. OUR**

The complete word is SOURCE.

**6. MAD**

The complete word is REMADE.

**7. potato**

The other three can be eaten raw.

**8. muse**

The other three mean 'investigate'.

**9. kangaroo**

The other three are members of the horse family.

**10. detached**

The other three mean 'to have set-off'.

**11. adjust**

The other three mean 'to keep someone or something within a certain area'.

**12. cinema**

The other three are parts of a story.

**13. decline**

'growth' means 'an increase', whereas 'decline' means 'a decrease'.

**14. massive**

'tiny' means 'very small', whereas 'massive' means 'very large'.

**15. straighten**

'bend' means 'to make something curve', whereas 'straighten' means 'to make straight'.

**16. loathing**

'adoration' means 'a strong love and respect', whereas 'loathing' means 'hatred'.

**17. clean**

'polluted' can mean 'made unclean by harmful substances', whereas 'clean' means 'free from dirt'.

**18. replace**

'remove' means 'to take something away', whereas 'replace' means 'to put something back'.

**19. embarrassed**

'unashamed' means 'to feel or show no shame ', whereas 'embarrassed' can mean 'to feel or show shame'.

**20. nimble**

Both words mean 'able to move quickly and easily'.

**21. toxin**

Both words mean 'something that can harm the harm the body'.

**22. reserved**

Both words mean 'arranged something to use in the future'.

**23. bandit**

Both words mean 'thief'.

**24. waver**

Both words mean 'to quiver'.

**25. skirmish**

Both words mean 'a short battle'.

# Test 19 — pages 58-69

**1. toughen**

'soften' means 'to make less hard', whereas 'toughen' means 'to harden and make stronger'.

**2. slanted**

'level' means 'straight', whereas 'slanted' means 'sloping'.

**3. large**

'slight' means 'small', whereas 'large' means 'big'.

**4. restrain**

'unbind' means 'to untie or release someone', whereas 'restrain' means 'to stop someone from moving'.

**5. unloving**

'affectionate' means 'loving', whereas 'unloving' means 'not loving'.

**6. blot**

'blot' can mean 'a smudge or blemish' or 'to sponge up a liquid'.

**7. path**

'path' can mean 'a footway for pedestrians' or 'a direction of travel'.

**8. fill**

'fill' can mean 'to block up' or 'to make something become full'.

**9. stunt**

'stunt' can mean 'to slow something down' or 'an impressive and exciting action'.

**10. fold**

'fold' can mean 'a line formed when something is folded' or 'to hold lovingly in your arms'.

**11. apologise**

'apologise' means 'to say sorry'.

**12. breakable**

'breakable' means 'easily broken'.

**13. citizen**

'citizen' means 'a member of a country'.

**14. propel**

'propel' means 'to drive forward'.

**15. collision**

'collision' means 'things crashing together'.

**16. imitate**

'mimic' and 'imitate' both mean 'copy someone or something'.

**17. supervise**

'oversee' and 'supervise' both mean 'to manage'.

**18. atrocious**

'horrible' and 'atrocious' both mean 'very unpleasant'.

**19. union**

'alliance' and 'union' both mean 'a joining together of separate things'.

**20. dwelling**

'residence' and 'dwelling' both mean 'a home'.

**21. ravenous**

'hungry' and 'ravenous' both mean 'to feel a need for food'.

**22. catastrophe**

'tragedy' and 'catastrophe' both mean 'a disaster'.

**23. object**

'oppose' and 'object' both mean 'to show disagreement'.

**24. evacuate**

'leave' and 'evacuate' both mean 'to depart from a place'.

**25. genius**

'mastermind' and 'genius' both mean 'a very intelligent person'.

## Puzzles 7 — page 60

### The Jumbled Sea

The unscrambled words are: SEAL, CRAB, SHARK, WHALE, TURTLE, DOLPHIN, SEAGULL, GOLDFISH, CROCODILE

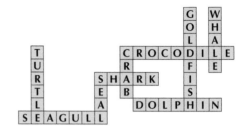

 © CGP — not to be photocopied

# Test 20 — pages 61-63

**1. expulsion**
'admission' means 'letting someone in', whereas 'expulsion' means 'forcing someone out'.

**2. separate**
'merge' means 'to come together', whereas 'separate' can mean 'to part'.

**3. appreciative**
'ungrateful' means 'not showing thankfulness', whereas 'appreciative' means 'showing thankfulness'.

**4. popular**
'disliked' means 'not liked', whereas 'popular' means 'liked'.

**5. peaceable**
'aggressive' can mean 'likely to act violently', whereas 'peaceable' means 'likely to avoid violence'.

**6. few**
'numerous' means 'many', whereas 'few' means 'not many'.

**7. male**
'male' makes sense here — it is the word that means 'to do with men', whereas 'mail' means 'items of post'.

**8. lava**
'lava' makes sense here — it is the word that means 'liquid rock from a volcano', whereas 'larva' means 'a young insect'.

**9. colonel**
'colonel' makes sense here — it is the word that means 'a leader in an army', whereas 'kernel' means 'the centre'.

**10. faint**
'faint' makes sense here — it means 'likely to collapse', whereas 'feint' means 'an action designed to mislead'.

**11. hauls**
'hauls' makes sense here — it is the word that means 'drags', whereas 'halls' is the plural of the word 'hall'.

**12. style**
'style' makes sense here — it is the word that means 'a way of doing something', whereas 'stile' means 'a structure with steps that helps you to climb over something'.

**13. evil**
Both words mean 'wicked'.

**14. swell**
Both words mean 'to increase in size'.

**15. unhappy**
Both words mean 'sad'.

**16. gather**
Both words mean 'come together over time'.

**17. outstanding**
Both words mean 'very good'.

**18. supplies**
Both words mean 'items that will be used for a specific task'.

**19. encourage**
Both words mean 'push someone to do something'.

**20. ARM**
The complete word is CHARMING.

**21. ARE**
The complete word is SCARES.

**22. OAK**
The complete word is CLOAKS.

**23. ONE**
The complete word is THRONES.

**24. FIN**
The complete word is DEFINE.

**25. OWE**
The complete word is STOWED.

# Test 21 — pages 64-66

**1. lifeless**
'spirited' means 'full of energy', whereas 'lifeless' means 'lacking energy'.

**2. unnerve**
'reassure' can mean 'to remove someone's fears', whereas 'unnerve' can mean 'to make someone feel afraid'.

**3. doubt**
'trust' means 'to feel sure about something', whereas 'doubt' means 'to feel unsure about something'.

**4. vend**
'buy' means 'to purchase', whereas 'vend' means 'to sell'.

**5. familiar**
'unknown' can mean 'not known to someone', whereas 'familiar' means 'known to someone'.

**6. criminal**
'lawful' means 'following the law', whereas 'criminal' means 'against the law'.

**7. motivation**
Both words mean 'a reason for doing something'.

**8. sparse**
Both words mean 'in short supply'.

**9. settlement**
Both words mean 'a place where a community of people lives'.

**10. demand**
Both words mean 'something that is required'.

**11. immediate**
Both words mean 'done at once'.

**12. barrier**
Both words mean 'something that is in the way'.

**13. fortress**
Both words mean 'a building which has been fortified'.

**14. waterbird**
A 'goose' is a 'waterbird' — a 'waterbird' is a bird which spends most of its time around water.

**15. post**

A 'parcel' is a type of 'post' — 'post' is anything that comes in the mail.

**16. weapon**

A 'missile' is a 'weapon' — a missile is a weapon that flies through the air or water.

**17. pastry**

An 'eclair' is a 'pastry' — it has cream inside it.

**18. room**

A 'library' is a 'room' — it's a room where books are stored.

**19. crime**

'theft' is a 'crime' — it's an act which is against the law.

**20. warrior**

'warrior' means 'someone who fights'.

**21. refuge**

'refuge' means 'a place of safety'.

**22. reinforce**

'reinforce' means 'to strengthen'.

**23. stagnant**

'stagnant' means 'still and foul'.

**24. fixated**

'fixated' means 'to be obsessed with'.

**25. desire**

'desire' means 'to want something'.

## Test 22 — pages 67-69

**1. fly**

The other three are noises.

**2. trickery**

The other three mean 'a lie'.

**3. corridor**

The other three are things you use to enter a place.

**4. conductor**

The other three are musical instruments.

**5. pilot**

The other three are parts of a plane.

**6. awe**

The other three refer to being angry.

**7. jackpot**

'jackpot' is the only correctly spelled word that can be made.

**8. watchtower**

'watchtower' is the only correctly spelled word that can be made.

**9. handsome**

'handsome' is the only correctly spelled word that can be made.

**10. tablespoon**

'tablespoon' is the only correctly spelled word that can be made.

**11. standstill**

'standstill' is the only correctly spelled word that can be made.

**12. lifeguard**

'lifeguard' is the only correctly spelled word that can be made.

**13. lawbreaker**

A 'vandal' is a 'lawbreaker' — it is someone who destroys or damages someone else's property.

**14. furniture**

A 'recliner' is a type of 'furniture' — it is something you can sit on.

**15. spice**

'cinnamon' is a spice — it is used to add flavour to food.

**16. artist**

A 'sculptor' is an 'artist' — it is someone who makes art by carving materials.

**17. device**

A 'laptop' is a 'device' — it is a portable computer.

**18. container**

A 'flask' is a 'container' — it is something you keep liquid in.

**19. leader**

A 'president' is a 'leader' — it is someone who leads a country.

**20. zealous**

'unenthusiastic' means 'not showing enthusiasm', whereas 'zealous' means 'showing lots of enthusiasm'.

**21. delightful**

'revolting' means 'disgusting', whereas 'delightful' means 'pleasant'.

**22. discord**

'harmony' means 'things working well together', whereas 'discord' means 'disagreement'.

**23. export**

'import' means 'to bring in things from another country', whereas 'export' means 'to send things to another country'.

**24. miniscule**

'vast' means 'large', whereas 'miniscule' means 'very small'.

**25. modestly**

'grandly' can mean 'in a rich and impressive way', whereas 'modestly' can mean 'in a small and low-key way'.

## Puzzles 8 — page 70

### Marvellous Maps

The correct coordinates are:
( E , 4 ) , ( A , 5 ) , ( H , 3 ) , ( B , 3 ) , ( C , 6 ).
The treasure is buried at the **BEACH** in square ( D , 1 ).

© CGP — not to be photocopied

# Test 23 — pages 71-73

**1. flaw**
'flaw' makes sense here — it is the word that means 'fault', whereas 'floor' means 'a surface to stand on'.

**2. side**
'side' makes sense here — it is the word that means 'edge', whereas 'sighed' means 'a long exhale'.

**3. story**
'story' makes sense here — it is the word that means 'a tale', whereas 'storey' means 'a level of a building'.

**4. mussels**
'mussels' makes sense here — they are a type of seafood, whereas 'muscles' are parts of the body that help control movement.

**5. hanger**
'hanger' makes sense here — it means 'something that clothes are hung from', whereas 'hangar' means 'a building for storing aircraft'.

**6. whether**
'whether' makes sense here — it is the word that means 'to show doubt about something', whereas 'weather' means 'the conditions outside'.

**7. beam**
'beam' can mean 'a stream of light ' or 'a long, thick bit of wood'.

**8. entertain**
'entertain' can mean 'to give someone enjoyment' or 'to hold an event'.

**9. flash**
'flash' can mean 'to light up suddenly' or 'to move very quickly'.

**10. cause**
'cause' can mean 'a reason for doing something' or 'to make something happen'.

**11. lead**
'lead' can mean 'a helpful piece of information' or 'to direct'.

**12. mount**
'mount' can mean 'to get bigger' or 'go up on to'.

**13. defend**
'assault' means 'attack', whereas 'defend' means 'protect from an attack'.

**14. central**
'outlying' means 'on the outskirts', whereas 'central' means 'in the middle'.

**15. cheerful**
'woeful' means 'sad', whereas 'cheerful' means 'upbeat'.

**16. dawdle**
'hasten' means 'hurry', whereas 'dawdle' means 'take your time'.

**17. generously**
'stingily' means 'giving away reluctantly', whereas 'generously' means 'giving away happily'.

**18. allowed**
'forbidden' means 'not permitted', whereas 'allowed' means 'permitted'.

**19. imaginary**
'imaginary' makes sense here — 'fictional' and 'imaginary' both mean 'made up'.

**20. tramped**
'tramped' makes sense here — 'stamped' and 'tramped' both mean 'walk heavily and noisily'.

**21. obviously**
'obviously' makes sense here — 'clearly' and 'obviously' both mean 'in a way that is plain to see'.

**22. harassed**
'harassed' makes sense here — 'pestered' and 'harassed' both mean 'annoyed with repeated questions'.

**23. tiresome**
'tiresome' makes sense here — 'boring' and 'tiresome' both mean 'dull'.

**24. inelegantly**
'inelegantly' makes sense here — 'awkwardly' and 'inelegantly' both mean 'in a clumsy way'.

**25. soothing**
'soothing' makes sense here — 'relaxing' and 'soothing' both mean 'peaceful'.

# Test 24 — pages 74-76

**1. wretched**
Both words mean 'very sad'.

**2. reckless**
Both words mean 'without thinking of the consequences'.

**3. delight**
Both words mean 'to please someone'.

**4. reveal**
Both words mean 'to give up information that was secret'.

**5. worrying**
Both words mean 'causing worry or concern'.

**6. devise**
Both words mean 'to come up with something'.

**7. stride**
'stride' means 'to take large steps'.

**8. monarch**
'monarch' means 'a ruler of a country'.

**9. flimsy**
'flimsy' means 'easy to damage'.

**10. conspire**
'conspire' means 'to plot together'.

**11. forecast**
'forecast' means 'to predict'.

**12. rant**
'rant' means 'an angry speech'.

**13. motivate**
'dispirit' means 'discourage', whereas 'motivate' means 'encourage'.

**14. disguise**
'expose' means 'reveal', whereas 'disguise' means 'conceal'.

**15. well**
'unhealthy' means 'not healthy', whereas 'well' means 'healthy'.

**16. unmindful**
'heedful' means 'aware of things', whereas
'unmindful' means 'unaware of things'.

**17. squander**
'save' means 'to keep something', whereas 'squander'
means 'to use something wastefully'.

**18. imperfect**
'flawless' means 'perfect', whereas 'imperfect' means 'flawed'.

**19. dismantle**
'build' means 'construct', whereas 'dismantle' means 'take apart'.

**20. HAT**
The complete word is SHATTERED.

**21. INK**
The complete word is BLINKING.

**22. HAM**
The complete word is SHAMELESS.

**23. OWN**
The complete word is FROWNS.

**24. OWL**
The complete word is BOWLERS.

**25. ARM**
The complete word is CHARMS.

# Test 25 — pages 77-78

**1. start**
'start' can mean 'set going' or 'make a sudden movement'.

**2. roll**
'roll' can mean a 'a tube' or 'to move a wheeled object'.

**3. clash**
'clash' can mean 'a disagreement' or 'a clanging sound'.

**4. treasure**
'treasure' can mean 'to appreciate' or 'wealth'.

**5. end**
'end' can mean 'the tip of something' or 'the finish'.

**6. announce**
Both words mean 'to say something confidently'.

**7. combat**
Both words mean 'fight against'.

**8. suddenly**
Both words mean 'quickly and without warning'.

**9. bright**
Both words mean 'colourful'.

**10. model**
Both words can mean 'something that is designed
to show what something should be like'.

**11. indistinct**
'clear' means 'obvious', whereas 'indistinct' means 'unclear'.

**12. miniature**
'giant' means 'huge', whereas 'miniature' means 'very small'.

**13. lengthy**
'brief' means 'short', whereas 'lengthy' means 'long'.

**14. destruction**
'creation' means 'making something', whereas
'destruction' means 'destroying something'.

**15. enmity**
'friendship' means 'being friends', whereas 'enmity'
means 'being hostile to one another'.

**16. avoid**
'face' can mean 'deal with something', whereas
'avoid' can mean 'fail to deal with something'.

**17. courteously**
'rudely' means 'in an impolite way', whereas
'courteously' means 'politely'.

**18. innocently**
'guiltily' means 'doing something in a guilty way', whereas
'innocently' means 'doing something in an innocent way'.

**19. acknowledge**
'ignore' means 'to pay no attention to something', whereas
'acknowledge' means 'to notice and accept something'.

**20. chill**
'warm' means 'to heat up', whereas 'chill' means 'to cool down'.

**21. shelter**
A 'tent' is a 'shelter' — it is somewhere you can sleep.

**22. dance**
The 'tango' is a type of 'dance' — it is danced in pairs.

**23. business**
A 'bakery' is a type of 'business' — it is a shop
where you can buy baked goods.

**24. dream**
A 'nightmare' is a 'dream' — it is a bad dream.

**25. collection**
A 'cluster' is a 'collection' — it is a group of things.

# Puzzles 9 — page 79

**Word Maker**
outcast, inside, lunchbox, nighttime

**Shipshape Words**
BOAT — COAT — CHAT — CHAP — CHIP — SHIP

# Test 26 — pages 80-82

**1. ART**
The complete word is CARTON.

**2. MAR**
The complete word is SMARTER.

**3. AMP**
The complete word is CAMPERS.

**4. OIL**
The complete word is SPOILED.

**5. IMP**
The complete word is LIMPED

**6. OUR**
The complete word is TOURED.

**7. practical**
The other three can mean 'overdecorated'.

**8. tusk**
The other three are animals.

**9. recording**
The other three are types of artwork.

**10. knight**
The other three are objects carried by warriors in battle.

**11. liquid**
The other three are fluids made by the body.

**12. sprinting**
The other three are water activities.

**13. apt**
'unsuitable' means 'not appropriate', whereas 'apt' means 'appropriate'.

**14. resent**
'forgive' means 'stop feeling angry at someone', whereas 'resent' means 'feel bitter towards someone'.

**15. tighten**
'relax' can mean 'to loosen', whereas 'tighten' means 'to make more tight'.

**16. uneven**
'level' means 'even', whereas 'uneven' means 'not even'.

**17. misfortune**
'luck' means 'success that happens by chance', whereas 'misfortune' means 'problems that happen by chance'.

**18. difference**
'similarity' means 'a thing that is like another thing', whereas 'difference' means 'a thing that is unlike another thing'.

**19. expect**
Both words can mean 'to expect something to happen soon'.

**20. plague**
Both words mean 'a sickness'.

**21. repulse**
Both words mean 'to push something away'.

**22. adapt**
Both words mean 'to alter'.

**23. foolish**
Both words mean 'stupid'.

**24. talent**
Both words mean 'a natural skill'.

**25. devastate**
Both words mean 'to destroy'.

# Test 27 — pages 83-85

**1. peel**
'peel' makes sense here — it is the word that means 'remove the skin of', whereas 'peal' means 'ring loudly'.

**2. chilli**
'chilli' makes sense here — it is the word that means 'a spicy pepper', whereas 'chilly' means 'cold'.

**3. symbol**
'symbol' makes sense here — it is the word that means 'something that represents something else', whereas a 'cymbal' is a flat musical instrument made from brass.

**4. sole**
'sole' makes sense here — it is the word that means 'only', whereas 'soul' means 'spirit'.

**5. fir**
'fir' makes sense here — it is the word that means 'evergreen tree', whereas 'fur' means 'an animal's hair'.

**6. lesson**
'lesson' makes sense here — it is the word that means 'time set out for learning', whereas 'lessen' means 'to reduce'.

**7. comeback**
'comeback' is the only correctly spelled word that can be made.

**8. airline**
'airline' is the only correctly spelled word that can be made.

**9. override**
'override' is the only correctly spelled word that can be made.

**10. sunroof**
'sunroof' is the only correctly spelled word that can be made.

**11. washer**
'washer' is the only correctly spelled word that can be made.

**12. goodwill**
'goodwill' is the only correctly spelled word that can be made.

**13. pleased**
'dissatisfied', means 'unhappy', whereas 'pleased' means 'happy'.

**14. misery**
'joy' means 'happiness', whereas 'misery' means 'unhappiness'.

**15. courage**
'cowardice' means 'a lack of bravery', whereas 'courage' means 'bravery'.

**16. secure**

'unguarded' means 'not protected or guarded',
whereas 'secure' means 'safe'.

**17. critical**

'complimentary' means 'praising', whereas
'critical' means 'finding fault'.

**18. recover**

'sicken' means 'get ill', whereas 'recover' can mean 'get better'.

**19. include**

'omit' means 'leave out', whereas 'include' means 'put in'.

**20. anxious**

'anxious' makes sense here — 'uneasy' and
'anxious' both mean 'nervous'.

**21. shielded**

'shielded' makes sense here — 'protected' and
'shielded' both mean 'defended from harm'.

**22. faultless**

'faultless' makes sense here — 'impeccable'
and 'faultless' both mean 'perfect'.

**23. screeched**

'screeched' makes sense here — 'shrieked' and 'screeched'
both mean 'cried out in a high-pitched voice'.

**24. investigate**

'investigate' makes sense here — 'examine' and
'investigate' both mean 'check thoroughly'.

**25. staring**

'staring' makes sense here — 'gazing' and
'staring' both mean 'looking steadily'.

## Puzzles 10 — page 86

**Precarious Parcel**

The words are: STABLE, ROOTED, COMPOSED,
ANCHORED, IMMOVABLE, FIXED, POISED, STEADY
Bobbi feels: SHAKEN

## Test 28 — pages 87-89

**1. punctuation**

A 'colon' is 'a type of punctuation'.

**2. sense**

'sight' is a 'sense' — it is one of the five senses.

**3. flower**

'poppy' is a type of 'flower' — it has red petals.

**4. shoreline**

A 'beach' is a 'shoreline' — a 'shoreline' is
where a body of water meets land.

**5. experiment**

'trial' and 'experiment' both mean 'test'.

**6. whirl**

'spin' and 'whirl' both mean 'to turn in a circular movement'.

**7. minimise**

'reduce' and 'minimise' both mean 'to make smaller'.

**8. emotional**

'sentimental' and 'emotional' both mean 'having strong feelings'.

**9. puncture**

'pierce' and 'puncture' both mean 'to go through something'.

**10. last**

'ultimate' and 'last' both mean 'final'.

**11. unafraid**

'fearless' and 'unafraid' both mean 'not showing fear'.

**12. illogical**

'nonsensical' and 'illogical' both mean 'lacking sense'.

**13. annoyance**

'nuisance' and 'annoyance' both mean 'something annoying'.

**14. faction**

'group' and 'faction' both mean 'an organised group of people'.

**15. rule**

'rule' means 'a regulation'.

**16. intercept**

'intercept' means 'to cut off or obstruct'.

**17. outlawed**

'outlawed' means 'made against the law'.

**18. breakthrough**

'breakthrough' means 'a sudden development'.

**19. illuminate**

'illuminate' means 'to shine a light on'.

**20. unworthy**

'deserving' means 'worthy of being treated a certain way',
whereas 'unworthy' means 'not deserving respect'.

**21. excessive**

'inadequate' means 'not enough', whereas
'excessive' means 'too much'.

**22. systematic**

'random' means 'illogical', whereas 'systematic' means 'logical'.

120

© CGP — not to be photocopied

**23. disengage**

'connect' means 'to join together', whereas 'disengage' means 'to separate from something'.

**24. complexity**

'simplicity' means 'being simple', whereas 'complexity' means 'being complicated'.

**25. assembling**

'dismantling' means 'taking apart', whereas 'assembling' means 'putting together'.

# Test 29 — pages 90-92

**1. education**

The other three are subjects taught in school.

**2. engineer**

The other three are circus performers.

**3. dolphin**

The other three are land animals.

**4. bland**

The other three mean 'unwilling to do work or use energy.'

**5. hatchet**

The other three can be used to reach a different level.

**6. seaweed**

The other three are sea creatures that have a shell.

**7. cut**

'cut' can mean 'to cut up' or 'an injury'.

**8. reservation**

'reservation' can mean 'an uncertainty about something' or 'an arrangement where something is reserved to use later'.

**9. pitched**

'pitched' can mean 'threw a ball' or 'put something up'.

**10. channel**

'channel' can mean 'a passage for liquids to flow along' or 'to direct through something'.

**11. incline**

'incline' can mean 'a surface that has one end higher than the other' or 'to bend your head forward'.

**12. wash**

'wash' can mean 'clean yourself' or 'remove dirt from clothes'.

**13. outer**

'interior' means 'on the inside', whereas 'outer' means 'on the outside'.

**14. unfairness**

'justice' means 'fairness', whereas 'unfairness' means 'a lack of fairness'.

**15. continue**

'cease' can mean 'to stop doing', whereas 'continue' can mean 'to carry on with'.

**16. unlucky**

'fortunate' means 'lucky', whereas 'unlucky' means 'not lucky'.

**17. harsh**

'mild' means 'not severe or intense', whereas 'harsh' means 'severe and intense'.

**18. controllable**

'unmanageable' means 'difficult to control', whereas 'controllable' means 'can be controlled'.

**19. acceptance**

'rejection' can mean 'saying no to something', whereas 'acceptance' can mean 'saying yes to something'.

**20. loosened**

'loosened' makes sense here — 'slackened' and 'loosened' both mean 'to make less tight'.

**21. exceptional**

'exceptional' makes sense here — 'phenomenal' and 'exceptional' both mean 'excellent'.

**22. pointless**

'pointless' makes sense here — 'useless' and 'pointless' both mean 'not having much purpose'.

**23. disadvantageous**

'disadvantageous' makes sense here — 'unfavourable' and 'disadvantageous' both mean 'likely to lead to problems'.

**24. tranquil**

'tranquil' makes sense here — 'restful' and 'tranquil' both mean 'calm and relaxed'.

**25. manoeuvring**

'manoeuvring' makes sense here — 'navigating' and 'manoeuvring' both mean 'steer skilfully'.

# Puzzles 11 — page 93

## The Great Swim

The correct words are: SEA, OCEAN, LAKE, RIVER, POND, STREAM, BROOK, PUDDLE

## Across Words

The pink flamin**go t**ried to steal our camera.

Victory was clinched thanks to Joe's go**al l**ate in the game.

Studying the tex**t he**lped Maria appreciate the story more.

Chi lifted the sword so high th**at e**veryone could see it.

## Test 30 — pages 94-96

**1. IRK**
*The complete word is SMIRKING.*

**2. TOR**
*The complete word is STORED.*

**3. ASH**
*The complete word is GASHES.*

**4. OWE**
*The complete word is COWERED.*

**5. AIR**
*The complete word is REPAIRED.*

**6. OLD**
*The complete word is BOLDER.*

**7. cereal**
*'cereal' makes sense here — it is the word that means 'a breakfast food', whereas 'serial' means 'happening in a series'.*

**8. bridle**
*'bridle' makes sense here — it means 'straps to lead a horse', whereas 'bridal' means 'to do with a bride or wedding'.*

**9. sells**
*'sells' makes sense here — it means 'gives things in exchange for money', whereas 'cells' means 'rooms in a prison'.*

**10. sought**
*'sought' makes sense here — it is the word that means 'looked for', whereas 'sort' means 'type'.*

**11. bread**
*'bread' makes sense here — it is the word that describes baked dough, whereas 'bred' means 'reproduced'.*

**12. wear**
*'wear' makes sense here — it means 'have something on your body', whereas 'where' is used to refer to the place where something is located.*

**13. courtesy**
*'rudeness' means 'a lack of politeness', whereas 'courtesy' means 'politeness'.*

**14. unconcerned**
*'distressed' means 'bothered', whereas 'unconcerned' means 'not bothered'.*

**15. scorching**
*'icy' means 'very cold', whereas 'scorching' means 'very hot'.*

**16. confidential**
*'public' means 'done in the open', whereas 'confidential' means 'meant to be kept a secret'.*

**17. extravagant**
*'thrifty' means 'uses money or supplies carefully', whereas 'extravagant' means 'uses up money and supplies freely'.*

**18. unethical**
*'right' can mean 'good', whereas 'unethical' means 'bad'.*

**19. construct**
*Both words can mean 'to create'.*

**20. upbeat**
*Both words can mean 'cheery and hopeful'.*

**21. imprison**
*Both words mean 'to lock someone up'.*

**22. intelligence**
*Both words mean 'cleverness'.*

**23. cautious**
*Both words mean 'does things carefully'.*

**24. inspect**
*Both words mean 'look at something very carefully'.*

**25. designs**
*Both words mean 'drawings or documents that show how something is going to be achieved'.*

## Test 31 — pages 97-99

**1. studious**
*Both words mean 'spends lost of time studying'.*

**2. appoint**
*Both words mean 'to assign someone to do something'.*

**3. insufficient**
*Both words mean 'not enough'.*

**4. bashful**
*Both words mean 'nervous around other people'.*

**5. frankness**
*Both words mean 'truthfulness'.*

**6. manipulate**
*Both words mean 'influence someone'.*

**7. craftsman**
*'craftsman' is the only correctly spelled word that can be made.*

**8. something**
*'something' is the only correctly spelled word that can be made.*

**9. farewell**
*'farewell' is the only correctly spelled word that can be made.*

**10. dumbstruck**
*'dumbstruck' is the only correctly spelled word that can be made.*

**11. armpit**
*'armpit' is the only correctly spelled word that can be made.*

**12. bagpipes**
*'bagpipes' is the only correctly spelled word that can be made.*

**13. swamp**
*'swamp' can mean 'an area of wet and boggy land' or 'to overwhelm completely'.*

**14. lies**
*'lies' can mean 'untruths' or 'to get in a resting position'.*

**15. drop**
*'drop' can mean 'a small ball of liquid' or 'to fall downwards'.*

### 16. shadow
'shadow' can mean 'to pursue someone without being noticed' or 'an area of darkness'.

### 17. burden
'burden' can mean 'a weight to be carried' or 'something that you are responsible for doing'.

### 18. answer
'answer' can mean 'give a response' or 'something that fixes a problem'.

### 19. clever
Both words can mean 'having original thoughts'.

### 20. engrave
Both words mean 'to carve text or a picture into something'.

### 21. happiness
Both words mean 'a feeling of joy'.

### 22. supply
Both words can mean 'to give something to someone that they need to perform a task'.

### 23. weakness
Both words mean 'a lack of strength'.

### 24. understate
Both words mean 'make something seem less than it is'.

### 25. taxing
Both words mean 'very tiring'.

## Puzzles 12 — page 100

### Wheel of Words

Possible answers may include:
RASH, RATS, REST, ROSE, ROTS
SEAR, SEAT, SHOE, SHOT, SOAR, SORE, SORT, STAR
HATS, HERS, HOSE, HOST
EAST, EATS, EARS
HASTE, HATES, HEARS, HEATS, HEROS, HORSE
SHARE, SHORE, SHORT, STARE, STORE
RATES, ROAST, ROTAS
TEARS, THOSE, TRASH
HEARTS, HATERS, HOARSE

### Problematic Palindromes

The word that can be viewed the same forwards, backwards and upside down is **NOON**.

© CGP — not to be photocopied

Answers

# Progress Chart

Use this chart to keep track of your score for each test.

| | Score | | Score | | Score |
|---|---|---|---|---|---|
| Test 1 | | Test 12 | | Test 23 | |
| Test 2 | | Test 13 | | Test 24 | |
| Test 3 | | Test 14 | | Test 25 | |
| Test 4 | | Test 15 | | Test 26 | |
| Test 5 | | Test 16 | | Test 27 | |
| Test 6 | | Test 17 | | Test 28 | |
| Test 7 | | Test 18 | | Test 29 | |
| Test 8 | | Test 19 | | Test 30 | |
| Test 9 | | Test 20 | | Test 31 | |
| Test 10 | | Test 21 | | | |
| Test 11 | | Test 22 | | | |

Look back at your scores once you've done all the tests. Each test is out of 25 marks. Work out which kind of mark you scored most often:

**0-15 marks** — Go back to basics and work on your question technique.

**16-20 marks** — You're nearly there — go back over the questions you found tricky.

**21+ marks** — You're a Vocabulary star. Go on to 10-Minute Tests for ages 10-11.